THROUGH

Hell

AND

High Water

A POLICE WIDOW'S STORY OF
TRAGIC LOSS AND REDEEMING LOVE

THROUGH

Hell

— AND —

High Water

A POLICE WIDOW'S STORY OF
TRAGIC LOSS AND REDEEMING LOVE

April Katherman-Redgrave

REDEMPTION
PRESS

Published by Redemption Press, PO Box 427, Enumclaw, WA 98022.

Toll-Free (844) 2REDEEM (273-3336)

Redemption Press is honored to present this title in partnership with the author. The views expressed or implied in this work are those of the author. Redemption Press provides our imprint seal representing design excellence, creative content, and high quality production.

ISBN 13: 978-1-64645-227-9 (Paperback)
978-1-64645-228-6 (ePub)
978-1-64645-229-3 (Mobi)

Library of Congress Catalog Card Number: 2021901540

Dedication

For my first love,
my husband in heaven, Mike.
I loved you yesterday. I love you still.
Always have, always will.

Contents

Acknowledgments

Without my faith in Christ, I wouldn't be where I am today. Thank You, Lord, for carrying my boys and me through hell and high water.

My husband on earth, David. Thank you for never believing my biggest fear, that the boys and I were too much. That our story, our baggage, and our broken hearts would be too much for any man to want to love. You have done more than just love the three of us. You have loved Mike as well. Your selflessness never ceases to amaze me. The way you always incorporate Mike into the family we have created together means more to me than I think you will ever fully know or understand. Thank you for loving my boys as your own. Thank you for loving all of me so well. My heart started beating again when I fell in love with you, and I will forever be grateful to God for blessing me with you. Thank you for always supporting my dreams and for being my biggest cheerleader through the journey of writing this book. I love the life we have created together. I love you *more.*

My boys, Josh and Jason. The two of you saved my life. I had nothing left in me when I lost your dad. My heart was shattered. You two were my reason to keep living. You gave me the strength to put those broken pieces back together and to live life in honor and remembrance of your dad. You are each like him in so many ways. I know with all my heart he is so proud of the two of you. I couldn't be prouder myself of the strong, wise, and resilient young men you have become.

My bonus son and daughter, Brayden and Tegan. You two have brought so much joy into my life. Thank you for welcoming me and the boys into your family, for sharing your dad with us, and for always loving Mike. Your huge hearts and unselfish willingness to always include him in our family mean the world to me.

And my daughter, Savannah. You are the cherry on top of this amazing story of love. You are truly my dream come true.

My family. Mom and Dad, my rocks who have been through hell and high water right along with me. Grandma and Grandpa, my biggest prayer warriors. Thank you all for teaching me what it really means to trust Jesus. Amber and Paulett, thank you for always being there for me, always supporting and always encouraging me.

Katherman/McHaffie/Banholzer family. Thank you for always being there for me and the boys, and for accepting David, Brayden, Tegan, and Savannah into your family with open arms and hearts.

Redgrave family. Josh, Jason, and I are so blessed to be a part of your family. Thank you for always showing your love and support to not only us, but always honoring Mike right along with us as well.

My friends. From losing Mike to losing our house to finding love again, my friends have supported me and the boys every single step of the way. Thank you for always being there, always showing up, and for never leaving us.

Acknowledgments

Lisa, your friendship through every stage in our lives has been a pillar of strength for me. Thank you for always encouraging, laughing with me, never judging, and constantly supporting me.

Morgan, thank you for taking such good care of me and the boys when I couldn't do it on my own. You have always been by my side, and I am beyond grateful for our special bond and friendship.

Heather and Natalie, thank you for always loving and supporting not only me but my whole family.

Derek and Anthony. You two accepted one heck of a job when you decided to be my family liaisons. Always looking out for and taking care of me and the boys when you were also mourning the loss of your friend. Even to this day, your dedication to Mike and our family continues, and I will be forever grateful.

My San Jose Police Department family. Your support and love from day one has never failed to continue year by year. Your commitment to honor your fallen brother and his family has been evident, and I can never thank you enough for all your support to me, Josh, and Jason. To my police wives: you are more than my friends—you are my sisters.

Concerns of Police Survivors (C.O.P.S.). Thank you for making it your mission to help in rebuilding the shattered lives of those who have lost a loved one in the line of duty. To all my survivor sisters and brothers, thank you for being a pillar of support, strength, and understanding.

I am forever thankful for the love and support of my pastors Malcom and Kathy MacPhail, my church family at New Hope Community Church, my community, and the countless prayer warriors who covered me and my family in prayer.

DreamPower Horsemanship. Thank you to Martha and her team for spending countless hours with me and the boys. Your selfless dedication has played a huge role in our healing process.

My talented and hardworking writing coach and editor, Jennifer. Thank you for pushing me and encouraging me to open my heart and write more than I thought I could. The Redemption Press team, thank you for having faith in me and encouraging me to share my story, God's story, through this book.

There are so many others who may not be acknowledged here yet have made an impact on my life. Please know you are not forgotten.

Chapter 1

--- ✦ ---

The Last to See Him, the First to Say Goodbye

The escort to the hospital seemed to take forever. No matter if we were driving Code 3, lights and sirens, I was never going to get to my husband fast enough. In my mind, I knew if I could just get to him in time, he would be okay. Nausea set in as we pulled into the hospital parking lot. We parked the car, and I suddenly began to shake and felt like vomiting. I wanted to get there so quickly, yet once we arrived, fear paralyzed me. I took a few deep breaths and nodded to the officer in the driver's seat that I was ready, even though I could never be ready for what I was about to face. I gripped the handle and opened the patrol car door to what was about to become my worst nightmare come true.

I slowly stepped out of the front seat and onto the asphalt parking lot of the hospital where my husband lay inside. My head was spinning. Panic overwhelmed me. Even though I knew in my mind he was already dead, my heart was not ready to confront my new reality. I had no clue what to expect once I had finally arrived. I still had no details as to what happened to him. I only knew he crashed on his police motorcycle. Was I going to see his body a mangled mess? Would there be blood? Where was he exactly? All I knew was I needed to get to him.

I shut the car door behind me and immediately noticed this was not the typical hospital parking lot scene I was stepping into. There were no people walking to and from their cars. In fact, there were hardly any other cars in the parking spots around us. Virtually no people to be seen anywhere. It was eerily silent all around me. I never felt more terrified, not knowing what I was about to face. I began the eerie walk, which will forever be etched in my mind, as if I were having an out-of-body experience watching a scene from a movie, with me as the main character.

The rest of the Regional Medical Center parking lot was filled with patrol cars. So many patrol cars. Like there was a big police emergency or event taking place. It took some time for me to realize the emergency, the event, was my nightmare. A perimeter of more patrol cars and officers set up around the hospital kept the media at bay. The media was waiting to get every detail they could on this breaking story taking place right before their eyes. What was a breaking story to them was my very life.

Derek, Mike's police academy mate and dear friend of our family, drove me to the hospital. I was grateful he was with me in that moment. The comfort and familiarity of his presence helped me to courageously face what I was about to walk into. I could almost feel the silence; it was thick in the air. It seemed to get thicker as I approached two walls of police officers in uniform. A sea of dark blue, San Jose Police Department patches, black boots, and shiny badges created a path to guide me into the side door of the hospital.

I walked through the officer-lined path, and not one officer gave me any sort of eye contact. It was as if I were on a conveyor belt, drifting past each officer one by one. Men and women, who were ordinarily strong and tough on the exterior, now stood with heads hung, tears streaming down their faces, whispering, "I am so sorry." Once I arrived at the end of that tear-stained path, the side door of the hospital was opened for me. I walked through the door like I was entering another realm where time stands still. It felt as if everything and everyone stopped that moment I crossed the threshold. The cold and sterile hallway was frozen in time for me to make my way deeper into my nightmare.

Nurses stopped and remained still at their stations. Officers in uniform and some in plain clothes stood at attention as I gradually moved down the hallways. So many officers had left their beats or families to pay respects to their fallen brother. Friends and family members lined the hallway as well. As I walked through the door, they froze. All eyes were on me. Deafening silence roared between beeps of hospital machines.

As I continued down the path toward the room my husband was in, I walked through a sea of silent sobs and whispers, which led me to a curtain. The only thing keeping me from finally seeing my husband was a white curtain hanging on silver round hooks. I remember hearing those metal hooks scrape against the metal bar they clung to as I slid it open, looking up to see the horror right before my eyes.

My legs shook and gave out beneath me, and I collapsed onto the cold, linoleum hospital floor. I was stuck. I couldn't move. I couldn't stand up, nor did I want to. I didn't want to look at him. I was afraid of what I was going to see. While on the ground I thought, *Why are there so many people here? How did they get here so quickly? So many people are staring at me, feeling sorry for me. Were they all told before me? Why am I the last one here? Wasn't I the first to know? How come everyone is already here surrounding Mike except for me?* This was the moment when I realized, *This is bad.*

Eventually, after what felt like many paralyzing minutes, my mother-in-law tenderly helped me to my feet. She walked me over to the side of the bed where my husband was. My beloved, my love, my life lay right there in front of me. He looked like he was asleep but in complete uniform. I wanted ever so badly to shake him awake and take him home. I wanted so badly for him to just be hurt and not dead. But he was already gone. He had been gone for hours, and I didn't make it in time for his last breath. I didn't get to hear his last words. He was already gone, yet he was right there in front of me.

So many people continued to enter the room; it was caving in. I wanted to crawl on the bed with him and make everybody leave. "Everybody, get out! Leave us alone! What are you even doing here?" I yelled in my head, but it didn't come out of my mouth. Instead, I just stood there in silence with all eyes on me.

There in the quiet, I placed his cold hand in mine and kissed it. I touched his pale, cool face with the back of my hand and stroked his cheek. Family members, officers, nurses, police command staff, my pastors—all of them tried to comfort me. Their hugs were suffocating; their words fell blank. All I could do was stare at my sweet husband lying lifeless in front of me. *Why are there so many people here?* I kept thinking.

Never letting go of his hand, and constantly stroking his

arm and kissing his forehead, I stood on his left side as my pastors and police chief stood on his right. The disheartening reality of what needed to come next was brought to my attention while I caressed my dead husband's dried, bloody hand. The media was waiting to release his name to the public. It needed to be done by the 8:00 p.m. news. *But I just got here! Everyone else had been here for God knows how long, but I just got here, and the media already gets to take control?* This meant I had to leave. My boys were at home unaware of what was going on. All they had to do to find out that their dad—their favorite person in life, their hero—was lying in a hospital bed dead and never coming home was turn on the news, get on their iPad, answer the phone of a frantic family member calling, or open the door to someone who rushed to our house. I would be damned if that were to happen. *Hell no!* The media wouldn't be releasing Mike's name on the 8:00 p.m. news without our precious sons knowing from me first.

It was a little after 7:00 p.m., and I wouldn't make it home by 8:00 p.m. even if I wanted to. No one in the room knew how furious I was for being the last to arrive, and now the first to have to leave. I wanted someone to flat out tell the media "No, you can wait." As much as I desired to shout out loud to everyone in the room, I calmly asked them to at least give me a few more minutes with Mike and time to get home to my boys. We agreed it would come out on the 9:00 p.m. news instead. It was not like the extra hour allotted me much more time, but it was a battle I had no energy to fight, nor did I even know how to at the time. It still didn't give me much more time with my husband either. How could they think a few extra minutes were enough?

I have never felt so torn. I wanted with all my heart to stay in that room next to him and never let go of his cold, rough, callused hand—the hand that was always warm, the hand that would engulf mine, the hand I had held since I was eighteen years old. I wanted everyone to leave so I could be alone with him. I hated I couldn't just throw myself on that hospital bed with him and sob in his arms. There were too many people shoved into every corner of the room and spilling into the hallway. I knew I needed to get home to my children soon, very soon. It is what he would have wanted me to do. He would have wanted me to get straight home to our boys.

Still with all eyes on me, I kissed his forehead wishing, just like the fairytale story our love was, my kiss would wake him up. I slowly let go of his blood-stained hand. I looked around at all the people who were getting to stay with my husband. *My* husband. I was mad. I was jealous. I didn't know at the time how bad leaving him that night would affect me.

My biggest regret was not speaking up and demanding more time with him. I wish I would have asked everyone to leave the room so I could have a moment with him alone. It wasn't fair. He was my everything, my world, my life. I had to leave my everything lying in a hospital bed so I could get to my children and beat the media. It will never be fair that I was the last to see him and the first to say goodbye.

Chapter 2

─────── ✦ ───────

What's Up, Ladies?

When I first saw Mike, he was driving a blue 1953 Willys military Jeep. We were in a Starbucks and Jamba Juice parking lot. This was a local hangout spot for college students. He was driving three other friends. The top was off, and they were yelling funny comments at people who were hanging outside through the PA system. It was the year 2000, one of our first nights of freshman orientation at Simpson College in Redding, California. Rebecca, Denise, and I lived only a few doors down from each other in our dorm and quickly became the best of friends. As the blue Jeep full of rowdy college boys pulled up to us girls, we heard, "What's up, ladies?" called out from the speakers.

This soon became Mike's tagline for my friends and me. He became known as the guy in the blue Jeep—the same blue Jeep the two of us eventually went on dates in. He would pick me up in front of my college dorm. He would have the top off, his arm resting over the back of the passenger seat ready for me to hop in with him. We would cruise around our little college town of Redding, and my hair would fly all over my face. He would look over at me, laugh, and drive even faster. Our date nights always ended with soft serve yogurt from TCBY. He would get chocolate and vanilla swirl with Reese's peanut butter cups, and vanilla with rainbow sprinkles for me.

This was also the same Jeep we would go four-wheeling in with no care in the world. I pretended to not be terrified and played it cool. He was fearless in that Jeep, and I was always waiting for us to tip over or get stuck. We never did. He handled the Jeep like a pro. Often when we went to his parents' house in San Jose, he would take me on the four-wheel trails in Hollister—the same trails we would go on years later with our two boys buckled in the backseat yelling, "Daddy, go faster!"

Little did we know he would eventually take our precious boys on ice cream dates, with the top down, and the wind flying through their hair. We spent our pennies keeping that Jeep running and in good condition. I still have this same blue Jeep, and our oldest son, Josh, hopes to fix it up and drive it as his own. That blue Jeep is where it all started.

Denise, Rebecca, and I, completely giddy by now, ended up following those cute college boys to Whiskeytown Lake. We hung out, joked around, and got to know each other better. That lake later became our usual hangout spot. A place where we could get off campus to get some freedom from the strict rules our Christian college had in place, take a break from our studies, and enjoy the sun and the water.

One part of this particular evening became a running joke throughout our marriage. Mike never let me forget the crush I had on his roommate. While Mike was trying to pick up on me that evening, I kept asking him questions about his roommate. After Mike and I were finally together, he would joke, saying he would tease me about that until the day he died. He definitely did, and I still laugh when I think about how adamant I was in trying to get Mike to put in a good word for me to his roommate when the whole time I was staring my future husband in the face. Before we knew it, what started with a goofy pickup line had blossomed into a friendship.

Mike and I were inseparable. We spent nearly all our free time together throughout the beginning months of our freshman year. Whenever my 1983 Ford Ranger pickup truck broke down—it always did—he was the one I called to come save me. This was the year 2000, and Mike still carried a huge pager clipped to the belt of his pants. He was who I paged with my own code so he knew it was me. He would call my prepaid flip phone and ask where I was, then quickly arrive with his tools to fix whatever was wrong under my hood and save the day. This happened often, and as bad as I always felt calling him for help, I soon realized he liked it when I needed him. This was the thing about Mike. He always helped people. He found joy and satisfaction from blessing others. It was something I soon found incredibly attractive about him.

Mike played on our college's basketball team. He was a five-foot-nine point guard with amazing hops and ball handling skills. Basketball was a passion of his and a sport I loved as well. I was a cheerleader in college, and as much as he teased me for it, he and I both knew he enjoyed having me there on the sidelines shaking my pom poms and cheering him on. After the games, I waited in the gym for him to come out of the locker room. Unfortunately, his basketball team our freshman year didn't have the best winning record, so I knew I would need to find a way to cheer him up. We usually ended up at the yogurt shop. Frozen yogurt typically did the trick to get his mind off a loss and back to his fun-loving self.

Mike was my go-to for just about anything. He was the guy I went to for my dating advice. I would tell him about my latest crush, and he would tell me why that guy wasn't good enough for me. When I came back to the dorms from a date, I would immediately go see him and tell him how it went. He always found something about my date to make fun of and make me laugh, which was one of the things he did best. He did this to the point where it would make me not like that guy anymore because I couldn't stop thinking about everything Mike said was wrong with him. I didn't realize his plan at the time. He was doing it on purpose because he had a crush on me and wanted me all to himself.

In October, during Columbus Day weekend, the two of us, one of his roommates, Marcus, and one of my good friends on my cheer team, Krista, decided on a whim that we wanted to get off campus for the three-day weekend. Where would we go? We were in Redding, a small town in Northern California, with not much to do, not much to see, and not too many places around we hadn't already explored. Without hesitation Mike said, "Let's go to my house! My parents will be totally cool with it." So the four of us went back to our dorm rooms, packed our weekend overnight bags, and in no time were in Mike's van ready for the four-hour road trip from Redding to his hometown of San Jose.

Along with the blue Jeep, Mike also had his parents' minivan on campus. As funny as it was to tease this cute college boy about driving a minivan, it became the go-to car we always piled our friends into to go places together. He also had a white hatchback volkswagon GTI and a plated dirt bike that could be ridden on the street. I would say to my girlfriends, "Who is this guy? What kind of college freshman has four vehicles to bring to college?"

I am still not even sure how he was allowed to have so many vehicles on campus, let alone as a freshman. The Jeep was the vehicle used to hit on chicks. The motorcycle, which we also still have to this day, was most likely thought to make him look cool, and the GTI was completely unnecessary, an ugly lowrider that I teased him for having. Yet it was the car, along with the van, that I ended up having to drive after we got married. I had no idea at the time I would end up inheriting all these vehicles I had teased him about when we first met.

The four of us had a great time on our road trip to San Jose. Mike drove, with Marcus in the passenger seat next to him. Krista and I giggled in the back seat of the van as Mike told us about his hometown and how cool he thought he was in high school. To me, San Jose was a big city. One I had never been to. I was a country girl from my tiny hometown of Gardnerville, Nevada, so big cities were both intimidating and exciting. As we got closer to San Jose, it became dark, and the city lights shone all around. I was in awe of all the lights and had never seen such a sight. I couldn't believe all the cars on the highways and never knew what true traffic was until that moment. Little did I know at the time that the city of San Jose would shape and define me. I would end up teaching at the very school he described to us on that road trip, and I would end up driving those highways every day on my commute.

Mike was right. His parents didn't mind that he had brought three tagalongs home with him for a three-day weekend—they loved it. Being newly empty nesters, they jumped at any opportunity to have a full house again. Their home was cozy and inviting. Mike's mom had rooms and beds set up for each of us. She immediately made us feel welcome and at home. The house was beautifully decorated. They were the best hosts with the most delicious cooking and some of the best chocolate chip cookies I've ever tasted. I could instantly tell where Mike got his kind heart, generosity, and easygoing personality. He was just like them.

I remember when we got to his house, Mike wanted to show me his room. I hesitated and asked his parents if I could go in there. I'm sure I seemed like an immature young girl, but I had come from a very strict household where boys were never allowed in my room. I was rarely ever alone with a boy unless, of course, I lied to my parents and told them I was with my girlfriends when I really wasn't. At the time I didn't realize what an impact my asking their permission to go into their son's room had on them. As the years passed, I didn't even remember asking! Then, at our rehearsal dinner the night before our wedding, Mike's dad shared this exact story and how much he appreciated the polite gesture.

That weekend road trip sealed the deal for me. If I didn't already know that Mike was generous, kind, incredibly funny, and a wholesome boy from an amazing family, it was all confirmed that weekend. The guy I had always viewed as my best buddy was turning into my new crush. He had this way of not just making me feel like he really liked me, but that he adored me. He would look into my eyes and pause, which made me feel beautiful. Even in a group of people, his attention was always on me. He had this gentleman-like way that made me feel comfortable, safe, and respected. I remember telling Rebecca in her dorm room one night after we all got back from going out together, "Mike is going to make one lucky girl so happy one day."

On November 21, 2000, while sitting on the couch in the lobby of my dorm, Mike asked me to be his girlfriend. He told me he knew from day one of meeting me that he was going to be with me. He was just waiting for me to realize it too. It took me four months to recognize this funny, big-hearted, basketball-playing buddy of mine was beginning to become more than a buddy to me. I had feelings for him all along; it just took me some time to realize it. I knew now I wanted to be the lucky girl he was going to make so happy.

This was the beginning of our love story. We dated all through college. He was not only my college sweetheart but also my first love—the only boy I had ever said "I love you" to. He was my best friend and my personal comedian. He could make me laugh like no one else. I had never been teased more in my life than by him, yet I loved it. His teasing came from a place of love, and it became one of the many aspects that made our love so unique and special. In fact, I'm sure he would be teasing me right now about being a nerd who wrote a book and how I should have expanded more on my crush on his roommate.

Simpson was a private Christian college, and the talk is that girls are there to get their MRS degree or ring by spring. Couples frequently get engaged and married. By the end of our junior year, most couples who had started dating after us were already engaged or married. My dad told me that I couldn't get married until I finished college. He also engrained in my mind, for which I will forever thank him, that I would remain pure until marriage, meaning no sex until we said, "I do." Mike and I both took courses in the summer and even packed on extra units each semester so we could graduate a semester early. We were determined to get married, for obvious reasons of course, but also because we knew without a shadow of a doubt that we were going to spend the rest of our lives together.

On my twenty-first birthday, four months before our college graduation, Mike proposed to me on the beach in Santa Cruz. A day I felt like I had waited so patiently and so long for. We were ready to begin another chapter in our young, madly-in-love, so-pure lives. I had found the one whom my soul longed for, and I was finally going to marry and spend the rest of my life with him.

Even if I had known that sixteen years later, the goofy, basketball-playing college boy driving a blue Jeep I fell in love with would be tragically killed and taken from me in an instant, I would still do it all over again. From November 2000 to June 2016, he loved me the way most women dream of being loved.

Chapter 3

---------- ⬗ ----------

Little Did I Know

The old saying of "time flies when you're having fun" couldn't be truer for Mike and me. Even though I felt like I had waited so long to marry this college sweetheart of mine, those four years of college and engagement flew by. We were having such a blast together. Once kids and careers came, life got super busy, and the years seemed to fly by even faster. With each year that passed, we continued to have fun in all we did. Mike was the one who created all the fun. His humor kept our marriage easy, our parenting exciting, and our everyday lives happy.

Sixteen pretty-perfect-to-me years passed by in a blink of an eye. Before I knew it, we were entering into another summer full of family adventures. We had multiple camping trips planned to different places all over California. We loved taking our toy hauler loaded with our dirt bikes out to the middle of nowhere. We would camp for days on end. One of our favorite family adventures was camping at Hollister Hills SVRA. Even though it was close to home, we still felt like we were getting away from everything and everyone. Our days consisted of dirt-bike riding, barbecuing, playing different card and board games, and late-night stargazing together by the fire. It was ultimate family time at its finest. Little did I know, the summer would be filled with many new adventures, just not the kind we planned on or would ever ask for. These new adventures would become my misery.

At the time, we were living in Hollister. We had recently purchased a fixer-upper farmhouse out in the country on a small piece of land. It was our own little slice of heaven. I was teaching elementary school while also finishing up grad school. Mike encouraged me to begin my master's degree program about two years prior. He knew I had a goal of moving out of teaching in the classroom setting and into administration. He believed in me more than I believed in myself. On June 13, 2016, I finished the program and received my master's degree in education with a concentration in curriculum and development. He was my biggest cheerleader every step of the long process. Little did I know, my dream of furthering my career in education would be crushed that very next day.

Now we were all out of school for the summer. I had just finished another school year of teaching second grade. Josh finished fourth grade and turned ten on May 30. Jason finished second grade, with me as his teacher, and had just turned eight on May 28. Mike and I had recently celebrated our twelfth wedding anniversary on May 29. May was a great month for us. We would always joke that this is what we get for me being a teacher and trying to plan a wedding and babies at the end of the school year so I could have the summer months off. We didn't realize it would all result in three days in a row. But they were our favorite three days full of back-to-back celebrations.

We are a baseball-loving family and big San Francisco Giants fans. Our yearly tradition in May was to splurge a little on good seats, skip school and work for the day, and go to a home game in San Francisco. I wish I could have stopped time that last time at the ballpark and soaked in every moment together. Little did I know, it would be the last time we would ever celebrate those special days together as our little family of four.

On Tuesday, June 14, 2016, we were all home together on this summer day. Mike was working a late day shift and didn't need to leave the house until about nine that morning. The four of us enjoyed a leisurely breakfast while we waited for the tile guys to show up for another day of work.

We were in the middle of remodeling the hall bathroom of our farmhouse. Mike had done all the demolition of the bathroom himself. He also had two cute little assistants who would help him demo every day after school. He was so great about including the boys in any hands-on project he was doing. They idolized their daddy. Spending time with him, no matter what they were doing together, was their favorite. Once the men arrived, Mike went into the bathroom to make sure they were set for the day. I specifically remember one of them asking what color grout he wanted, and I heard him tell them, "Whatever my wife wants!"

Once it was time for Mike to leave for work, he thanked the guys for their hard work. He hugged the boys, as he always did. He told them to be good for their mom, as he always did. He kissed me goodbye, as he always did. Looking so handsome in his uniform, he got on his police motorcycle and drove away.

The comforting roar of his engine could be heard for a while as he rode down our country road. That was the last time I would hear his motorcycle engine roar. Little did I know, that was the last time our boys would get a hug from their dad. If

I would have known this would be the last time I would get a kiss from my husband, I would have held him closer, longer.

The boys played outside on our property for most of the day. They shot their BB guns, rode their dirt bikes, and played basketball. I checked on them occasionally but spent most of my day inside with the workers. We would be leaving in a few days to go camping with our good friends, the Tassios, so I was texting with Jaimee about meals, making my lists, and getting our camping trip plans all set in place.

As we always did, Mike and I texted about the little things happening at home. We were texting about the camping details, and I kept him updated on the tile progress and how I had to call a plumber to fix a leak in the kitchen. I noticed at one point, as I continued to update him about the work on the house, he had stopped responding.

No biggie, I thought. That was totally normal. Sometimes it took him a while to respond to me, but he always did, once he got off the bike or finished with a call for service. This is why I didn't think anything of him not responding. I was ignorant that in those moments of texting my husband, he was fighting for his life. While I was patiently waiting on a response to my camping questions, he had met our Lord face to face. He was never going to answer my texts, ever again.

As the boys continued to play outside, I sat on the couch and browsed Facebook. I saw a post in my news feed that simply said, "Pray for the San Jose Police Officers." I thought it was a little weird. My nosey intuition continued to read the comments on the post. As I scrolled through them, I read a comment that said an officer was injured. Further down I read it was a motors officer who was injured.

There were not many motors officers in the department. *Mike was one damn good rider, so it couldn't be him,* I thought.

Yet still no response to my texts. I soon realized Jaimee had stopped texting me too. This was when I started to get worried. I was hoping it was only a coincidence.

I attempted to call him, and I texted a few of my police friends, but no one answered my calls or responded to my texts. *They all knew.* They all knew my husband was hurt, and some even knew he was already dead. Yet, I knew nothing. Finally, Morgan called me and told me it was Mike who the Facebook post was referring to, and she and Derek would be right over.

Derek and Morgan were and still are very close friends of ours. Derek and Mike met in the police academy. They continued to not only work on the streets of San Jose together but became great friends outside of work. They were dirt-bike riding and camping buddies, and Derek was and is still like a silly uncle to our boys. When Derek met Morgan, who at the time was a San Jose Police Department dispatcher, we instantly clicked, and she soon became one of my closest friends. Knowing they were heading over gave me comfort, yet also a sense of worry as I wondered why she said they would be right over. Why did they need to come in person and why so quickly?

I sat on my couch. I continued to scroll through my phone. I continued to call and text Mike with no response. I was still pretty calm because the awful thoughts of my husband possibly being dead hadn't crossed my mind yet. I kept thinking, *Stupid Mike crashed on his bike and probably broke his leg. Here we are in the middle of this remodel; we are supposed to go camping this weekend, and now he hurt himself? Great!* Selfishly, I was almost a little frustrated with him. It was just the beginning of summer. All our summer adventures were going to be canceled because Mike was hurt and would be recovering from some kind of injury. Maybe Morgan and Derek could take me to him. I began to pack a little bag for him thinking he may want to change out of his uniform and into something more comfortable. I knew how he hated being in his hot uniform longer than he needed to be and preferred some basketball shorts and a T-shirt.

Little did I know, he was never going to need the basketball shorts and T-shirt. If only it was just a broken leg. If only the worst that came out of it was a bathroom remodel postponement. If only the disappointment of canceling our camping trip was my only frustration. If only he had not died . . .

I let Josh and Jason continue to play basketball out in the backyard as I waited for Derek and Morgan to arrive. There was no need to let the boys in on what was going on. They would just worry about their dad and ask a ton of questions. It was just a broken leg anyway. At least I was still convincing myself of this scenario. I was not going to allow any other scenario to enter my head. There was no way anything more serious than possibly a broken leg could be wrong with my husband. I wouldn't be able to survive.

Derek and Morgan arrived a few minutes later. As I heard the car pull up our gravel driveway, I walked out our front door and down the sidewalk path. I immediately noticed Morgan was driving her car, and Derek had driven his take-home police car. When he stepped out of the car, I saw he was not in uniform, but plain clothes. I stopped walking in the middle of our sidewalk path. I was frozen in place and terrified as to what they were going to tell me.

The look on Morgan's face told me instantly it was bad. Then as Derek was slowly walking toward me he shook his head to signal the word *no*, confirming my biggest fear. I collapsed on our lawn. Morgan sat down next to me and wrapped her arms around me. I kept saying over and over to Morgan,

"What am I going to do? How am I going to live without him?" Then I paused because it suddenly hit me. "The boys. How in the world am I going to tell them?" This was the moment my worst nightmare had begun.

All I wanted to do was get the heck out of there and get to Mike. But I couldn't. Derek had been instructed by the police department not to let me leave for the hospital yet. Official protocol needed to take place, and that official protocol was on their way.

As we impatiently waited inside the house, the moment every law enforcement or military spouse fears was about to take place at my front door. The dreadful black cars arrived and parked on the street in front of our house. The car doors opened, and multiple men in suits stepped out of the first car and onto our grass. These men were the city of San Jose's mayor and a few city council members. The second car held the San Jose Police Department chief and the chaplain.

It wasn't too long before I heard the knock. These highly esteemed men had arrived to deliver the unbearable news to the new widow.

Derek opened the door and escorted them to the living room, where I sat on the couch. No tears—solely in a state of utter shock and disbelief. By now Morgan and my good friend Theresa were outside keeping the boys occupied in the backyard, so they would not witness the tragic scene being played out inside their adored home.

The single-file line of powerful men in suits stood shoulder to shoulder, perfectly still, in front of the distraught woman they had no business visiting. The police chief and the chaplain knelt in front of me, took my hands, and did their best to console me. These two men were sincere. These two men were as shocked and broken as I was.

As I looked up and saw the statue-like strangers who had been stripping the San Jose Police Department of resources, finances, and officers, I grew angry, and I remembered the words Mike had told me after he'd lost a brother in blue a year prior: "If I ever get killed in the line of duty, don't you ever let the mayor step foot in our home or attend any service of mine."

At that memory, it was as if I snapped out of my state of shock. I realized who was standing in my living room. "Get the hell out of my house!" I shouted.

Now all those in the room were in a state of shock because of my outburst. There was no calming me down. Because of this man, my husband's department was short staffed to the point of insanity. As a result of the asinine decisions he had approved, Mike's vacation time for that week was denied. There were simply not enough officers to cover the shifts. We were supposed to be out of town camping and enjoying our first week of summer as a family, but instead my husband lay dead in a hospital bed and we would be planning his funeral.

"I mean it—get the hell out of my house." I went on to tell everyone standing in my living room exactly what my husband asked of me and demanded they respect his wishes.

Just as the men in the suits had been escorted into my house, they were escorted out. I regained my composure, with only Derek and the police department representatives with me. I had waited long enough. All I wanted now was to get out of that house and get to my husband.

Chapter 4

The Proposal

My dream since I was a little girl had come true. A day I waited so long and patiently for had finally come . . . or so I thought. It was our Christmas break from college. I went back to my parents' house in Gardnerville, Nevada. Mike drove up from San Jose to visit me for a few days. Holiday breaks were the worst. With me in Gardnerville and him in San Jose, I always missed him like crazy.

One night we sat on the couch in my parents' living room opening presents. It was my mom, dad, sister, brother, me, and Mike. My sister, Amber, was in high school, and my brother, Luc, in junior high. Amber and Luc loved Mike and thought he was the funniest guy, which indeed he was. His funniness credibility was about to go up tenfold as they all watched me open my present from Mike.

He saved the best for last. It was a small, round floral ring box with a gold bow on top. I thought, *This is it. He's proposing to me right there in front of my family!* My heart began to beat out of my chest in excitement, and all the different steps of the wedding planning process I had dreamed about since I was a little girl flashed through my mind. *How romantic*, I thought. *I wonder if he already asked my dad.* I slowly lifted the lid off the pretty ring box. With a deep breath, I excitedly looked inside, and quickly realized there was no ring.

There was something else inside, but I was not quite sure what. I stuck my finger in and felt something gooey. I looked at the tip of my finger, and I yelled, "What is this, poop?" What looked like a mound of poop inside that tiny box was freshly squirted grease from a grease gun. I was thoroughly confused and immediately started crying. "Are you kidding me?" I jokingly punched him in his arm. By this time my parents and siblings were dying of laughter. Tears were flowing from them all as they couldn't control how hilarious they thought this was. "Why would you do this, Mike?" He was right there with them laughing uncontrollably.

He quickly realized he better do something before this went south and I got too mad. He handed me a folded-up piece of paper—two tickets to the musical *Grease*. *Grease* was my favorite movie. He got us tickets to see the musical *Grease* in Reno. The grease in the ring box was supposed to be my hint as to what the present was. It was never intended to be a proposal. There was no way I would ever have put two and two together, that the grease in the ring box and now all over my finger would represent tickets to the musical. This was a big gesture and thoughtful on his part because he hated *Grease* and hated musicals. I love them. I eventually wiped my tears, which were not caused by laughter like everyone else's. I hugged and thanked my still-boyfriend-not-yet-fiancé and started to finally laugh along with everyone else.

This was the kind of humor Mike had. Always making everyone laugh, and most of the time at my expense. I still have that box of grease. I keep it with all my jewelry. Anytime I see it, I laugh out loud as I remember such a precious night with Mike and my family. What I thought was a mean joke ended up becoming a memory we still laugh about today. It is a story I tell Josh and Jason often, and we all get a great kick out of it.

Two years later, my dream since I was a little girl was coming true. A day I waited so long and patiently for was finally here. And this time around, the proposal was real. Inside the black square ring box was no grease. Instead, inside was a gorgeous, diamond engagement ring that a young girl like me only dreamed of wearing. We had spent the day playing on the beach in Santa Cruz. We swam in the water (or should I say, he threw me in the cold water), tossed around the football, walked up and down the beach, and lay in the sun.

There were times throughout the day he was acting a little weird and off. He was always looking at the time even though we had nowhere we needed to be. He asked me the same questions over and over. "Are you sure you want to have dinner on the beach?" "Do you still want to barbeque hot dogs?" He also had this cross-body backpack he wore all day long. I teased him and called it his "man purse." He didn't ever wear it, so the fact that he wouldn't take it off was suspicious. I offered a couple of times to take it when he went to the bathroom, or suggested he take it off when we were playing in the ocean, but he refused. After knowing what his end-of-day plan was, I understood why he was so off. He was nervous, and my engagement ring was inside that man purse of his.

As the sun went down, he made a fire for us. We sat on a huge, washed-up log while we roasted hot dogs on sticks. We talked and laughed. We always laughed. He always made me laugh. At one point in the night, he turned away from me to look like he was stoking the fire. When he turned around, he was down in the sand on one knee. I sat on the log while he stuttered over his romantic words and asked me to be his wife. I wish I could remember what he said to me that night. Mike was far from romantic, so that was one of those rare moments in our lives. What I wouldn't give to go back there even just for five minutes.

Without any hesitation, and with tears in my eyes, I said yes! We heard cheers behind us from a group surrounding a fire further down the beach. He twirled me around as I hugged his neck and kissed him. No more fake proposals. This was the real deal, and I couldn't wait to become Mrs. Michael Katherman.

The ring was gorgeous. He'd picked out the diamond and designed the band, which was lined with more tiny square diamonds. I loved it.

After we ended our romantic night on the beach, we got back in the car to make the drive from Santa Cruz to San Jose. On the drive home, we made some phone calls because we couldn't wait to tell everyone the news. We called my parents. Of course, my dad already knew because Mike had asked for my hand in marriage the last time he had seen him, which neither my mom nor I knew about. They were both so excited for us. They loved Mike like their own son. We called his parents. I remember telling them on speaker, "We are getting married!" They knew of Mike's plans that day and were anxiously awaiting that exciting phone call.

This perfect day was my twenty-first birthday. It was August 10, and we were getting ready to go back up to Simpson

College to finish out our senior year. I couldn't wait to show off my new bling to my college girlfriends and tell everyone we were engaged.

We both graduated in December of 2003. While I was finishing my only and last semester of my senior year in college, late nights in my dorm room didn't consist of studying anymore but of wedding planning. A couple of my college girlfriends were engaged at the same time. We joked that we actually got our "rings by spring" and our MRS degrees. We originally had planned on getting married in August 2004, but neither of us could wait a whole year, so we bumped it up to May.

It was May 29, 2004. A Cinderella wedding, complete with the gorgeous gown; long, white gloves; a tiara; and even a horse-drawn carriage. We were in a stage in our lives when we still had our close friends from high school and our new friends from our college years, which meant a large wedding party. We had twenty-three of our closest friends and many family members make up our bridesmaids, groomsmen, candle lighters, flower girl, ring bearer, and ushers. We had an evening wedding and had not seen each other prior to the double doors of the church sanctuary opening.

There I stood holding on tight to my dad's arm, a veil covering my face as I stared down the aisle at the man of my dreams waiting at the altar for me with a huge smile on his face. Our eyes glued on each other as I walked down the aisle to my soon-to-be husband. Our ceremony was Christ-centered and included some incredibly special moments. One moment in particular was when we exchanged rings. Before Mike put my wedding ring on my finger, he first took off my purity ring. My parents had given me a purity ring when I was fifteen. It signified my purity until my wedding day, not having sex until marriage. I kept that vow to God, to my parents, to myself, and to Mike. During this part of the ceremony, Mike took my purity ring, walked down the steps of the altar, and handed it back to my dad. He walked back up the steps to me and slipped my wedding ring on my finger. I am not sure if many of the almost three hundred people in attendance really knew what this special moment represented, but we did, and it was a choice we made. We were very proud of the blessings that decision brought into our marriage.

After the ceremony, it was time to have some more fun and party at the reception. Once we were done taking pictures inside the church, we ran out the front doors of the church through a tunnel of our guests screaming and clapping in congratulations. At the end was a horse-drawn carriage waiting to take Cinderella and her Prince Charming to the ball. My dad surprised me. The ride in the carriage took us through our small town to the CVIC Hall, which was a gorgeous historic brick building located in downtown Minden, Nevada. Once we arrived, our guests were already there to welcome us, and the dinner and dancing began. It was a perfect day. We were so young, so in love, and unaware of what our future held.

We honeymooned in Maui. It was eleven of the most glorious days filled with a perfect mixture of exploring, adventure, relationship, and romance. It was our first trip ever alone without our friends or parents with us. We stayed in Kaanapali at the Whaler in a little condo on the beach. Mike had been to Maui many times with his family, but it was my first time to that island. He loved showing me around his favorite places.

Mike preferred to be out hiking and exploring, and I preferred to be lounging by the pool. One morning he had us wake up early to hike down into the Haleakala Crater. It was hot, it was long, and it was tiring. He was having the time of his life, and I was complaining the whole time. We joked the rest of the trip at how mad I was at him for making me finish that whole hike. The next time we went to Maui, the first thing he asked was, "Do you want to hike Haleakala?" I punched him in the arm. "Heck no, we are lounging by the pool!"

After our honeymoon in Maui, we came back to our little apartment in Santa Clara and began our new life as a married couple. We both finally felt like adults now living for the first time together in our own place. Our apartment was close to the police department and not too far from the school where I was teaching. I was eager to make this little apartment a home for us and quickly decorated it. Mike hated all things girly, so he wasn't too thrilled with my sunflower décor in the kitchen or my pretty beaded throw pillows on the couches. He drove me crazy picking off the beads and throwing them around the living room. He thought it was hilarious and knew exactly how to push my buttons, now just a memory to make me smile and giggle.

Mike began the San Jose Police Academy, and I began teaching third grade at Calvary Chapel Academy in San Jose. Mike graduated college with a bachelor's degree in business, but he knew this wasn't the career he wanted. He always knew he either wanted to go into the military or police work. He applied to many different departments in the Bay Area. God had a plan for him and his career to be at San Jose PD. After our first year as newlyweds, we were busy in our careers when we found out we were expecting. Our tiny, firstborn son, Joshua Alec, surprised us early and was born on May 30, 2006. We spent our second wedding anniversary in the hospital, completely googly eyed over our tiny baby boy.

When Josh was three months old, we bought our first home and moved to Hollister, California, about an hour away from our apartment in Santa Clara. We now had to commute to San Jose for work, but Mike liked being able to get away from the city when he wasn't working, and house prices were more affordable there. It was not long before baby boy number two, Jason Daniel, came on May 28, 2008, surprising us early again like his brother. Another wedding anniversary, our fourth, was spent in the hospital falling in love with our newest addition. As the years went on, the boys grew up quickly right before our eyes. Mike was the best hands-on dad and often would say that his dream of having two sons was fulfilled.

We were his world, and he always made that known to us and everyone else. He would brag about his boys. He was proud that his little boys were avid dirt-bike riders, fishermen, and basketball and baseball players, just like him. I was often told by other people how highly he spoke of me. I'll never forget a buddy of his at work telling me how a bunch of them were wide-eyed over a pretty woman they all saw. He said Mike looked at all of them and said, "I don't need to look. I have the most beautiful woman waiting for me at home." That's how he always made me feel, like I was the most beautiful woman in the world, his dream girl.

He rarely took any overtime shifts unless they were mandatory. He would rather be home with us. He took pride in his job as a San Jose police officer, but it didn't consume him or his life. We were his life. He put us first, us and the Lord. He truly lived out the epitome of a Christ-centered life, loving his wife as Christ loved the church and putting his family first.

His love for me and our boys showed even as he left for

work that morning of June 14, 2016. Little did we all know that would be the last day the boys and I had those strong arms engulf us with his hugs. The last time his lips would kiss mine or the top of the boys' heads. The last time they would hear those words that he always stressed to them, "Be good for your mom."

Chapter 5

---⬥---

Heaven Must Have Needed a Hero

Josh and Jason were still at home, clueless as to why their mom had left. Morgan and Theresa stayed with the boys when Derek and I left for the hospital. They played with the boys until my parents and grandparents could get there. I am so thankful for these two strong women and amazing friends who kept it together and made the evening feel like any normal evening for my boys. They didn't suspect anything was wrong when I left.

As Derek drove me back home from the hospital in his police car, I was in a daze. I sat there thinking, *How am I going to face Josh and Jason when I get home? How in the world am I going to tell their daddy isn't coming home from work tonight? How would I break it to them that they would never get another hug, kiss, or hear words of advice from their dad again? How would I ever tell them their dad is lying dead in a hospital bed?*

We arrived back to my house, and once we pulled into my driveway, I knew I had to face those two precious boys. I was dreading what I had to do next. I knew that what I was about to do would break their hearts. I was scared and nervous. I kept praying and asking God to give me the words because I just didn't have them. My words were going to shape the rest of their lives. It would be a moment they would never forget. A moment to be etched in their memory as most likely the worst day of their lives, as it was mine. I was going to be the one to cause that. It made me sick to my stomach, and my nausea came back. I am sure they assumed I would be coming back home with their dad. I walked through the front door of our perfect little farmhouse in a way that I never had before. I walked through that door a widow, not a wife.

This is one area where God's hand over our family was evident to me. I have no family who live near me. My sister, Amber, was the closest but still lived over an hour away in Pleasanton. The day before Mike was killed, Amber had given birth to a beautiful baby girl, Evelyn Mae. I had submitted that very last paper for my master's program in the morning and spent the whole rest of the day at the hospital anxiously awaiting the arrival of my new niece. Once she arrived, I got my snuggles in and made the drive back home to Mike and the boys. My parents and my grandparents had all traveled to the hospital for the big arrival. They were planning on staying a couple of days to help my sister with my nephew, Drake, her two-year-old son, who was now a big brother.

God planned that perfectly. Instead of my parents being over five hours away and my grandparents over three hours away on this horrific night, they were only one hour away. I am always amazed at God's timing and how He orchestrates things, but in this case, I was angry. He knew Mike was going to die that very next day after Evelyn was born. God knew that Mike would never get to meet his niece. How could God allow this to happen? I hate the part where God knew my husband would die. Yet, He brought me comfort. God knew I would need my family there with me that night, and I would need them there quickly.

My grandma and mom were sitting at my kitchen table when I walked in the door. They both got up immediately, wrapped their arms around me, and we all sobbed. Once I let go of their embrace, I looked down at my arms and told them his dried blood was all over me. I still had not washed it off, and I didn't want to.

Looking back, I wrote this in my journal. It took me months to be able to reflect back on those first hours and days:

Later that night I had to take a shower to wash his blood off my arms. That should never ever be something I should have to do. I didn't want to wash it off. I would have left his dried blood on me forever if I could. I collapsed on the shower floor as his blood, mixed with water rolled off me and the drain. I sobbed uncontrollably. I still can't get the way he looked out of my head. A little bit of the same, but with dried up blood on him, a little puffy and so white and pale. This is hell on earth. Absolutely, unfair hell. It makes no sense. I don't understand God's plan at all. Why me? Why did God choose my husband, my children? Why?

It's just not fair! I miss Mike like crazy. It physically hurts me. I miss him more and more every second.

I sat down at the table with the two of them to catch my breath before I knew what had to happen next. I knew I needed to tell Josh and Jason that their daddy was not coming home, but I had no idea how I was going to bring myself to do it. I knew it had to be me and only me.

By now the media had released Mike's name, and word was spreading like wildfire that he was gone. His face was plastered all over the internet and television. Thank goodness my dad and grandpa had been keeping the boys occupied out in the barn and away from any electronics. I took a deep breath, opened our sliding back door, walked down the steps and through the back of our property to the barn. This was one of the many solemn, terrifying walks I was about to face where I had to keep myself together for the sake of everyone else around me.

As I walked into our barn, I will never forget the scene before me. Two of the most influential men in my life, my dad and my grandpa, were playing pool with my boys. Josh and Jason were laughing and having a great time with not a care in the world. My dad and grandpa were able to make such a tragic evening calm and normal for my boys. They didn't suspect anything. They had no worries. I can never thank these two strong men enough for being pillars of support for Josh and Jason that night.

I told the boys I was back. I knew that all my dad and grandpa wanted to do in that moment was to embrace me, cry with me, and mourn the loss of their son and grandson. Yet, we all kept our composure for those two innocent little boys who were about to get the biggest blow of their lives. All I could do was pray in my head, over and over, asking the Lord to give me the right words to say to them. This conversation I was about to have with them will forever be etched in their minds. I had to do it perfectly right.

I asked the boys to come in the house with me. All of us walked back to the house together. We were keeping the biggest secret of our lives from Josh and Jason, and I couldn't keep it in any longer, as much as I wanted to. I wish I could have gone days, even weeks, without telling them. I wish I could have prolonged their innocence, yet it was not our reality. Our reality was that we were about to be known as the widow and children of fallen San Jose Police Officer Michael J. Katherman. We were no longer simply April, Joshua, and Jason Katherman.

I told the boys to come with me into their dad's and my bedroom. My parents and grandparents each gave me a look before I walked another long, terrifying walk, this time down the hallway and into our bedroom. Their look confirmed that they were praying for us. I instantly noticed Mike's shoes in the corner. His dirty clothes hanging off the hamper. His pillow that he would never lay his head on next to me again. All I wanted to do was throw myself on our bed and sob, but I couldn't. I had to break my boys' hearts instead.

I asked them to sit on the bed with me. The three of us sat together. I told them I needed to talk to them about their dad. Jason is just like his dad. He is a talk-before-he-thinks jokester, and he immediately said, "What, is dad dead?" with a little smirk. It took me a little while to catch my breath after his comment.

I went on to calmly ask the boys a series of questions:

"Who do you think is the best motorcycle rider at the police department?"

"Dad, of course!" they both replied.

"Who do you think is the bravest police officer at the department?"

"It's Dad."

"Who do you think is your biggest hero?"

"Dad." They both answered in unison.

"Well boys, Jesus thinks the same exact thing. He thinks that your dad is the best, bravest, and biggest hero there is. He needed another brave hero in heaven, so He decided out of all the officers at the San Jose Police Department, your daddy is the one He chose. Daddy got to go to heaven tonight to meet Jesus."

Our oldest son, Josh, at ten years old, looked as if he had seen a ghost. His sweet, high-pitched voice saying, "What?!" will forever be etched in my mind. He is my more sensitive one, and he immediately broke down in tears repeating the word *no* over and over.

Jason, at eight years old, who has a more laid-back personality, like his dad, and is not very sensitive, immediately looked around our bedroom and asked, "What are we going to do with all his stuff?"

I held Josh in my arms as I answered Jason's question. "We are going to keep it of course, all of it." The three of us sat on my bed together for quite some time. In my head, I thanked God over and over for giving me the words to say to these boys of ours. In that moment, I realized I had just done the hardest thing I had ever done as a mom and may ever do. I just told my sons their dad was dead. My husband of twelve years was never going to sit on that bed where I sat holding our brokenhearted sons ever again.

Once the boys and I came out of my bedroom and back into the living room where my parents and grandparents were, we were all in shock. No one really knew what to say, and we adults all felt the need to keep our feelings in check so as not to upset the boys. Soon I heard a car—it was Paulett and Mason. I ran out of the house when I heard their car and sobbed with Paulett. Paulett is my aunt and we grew up more like sisters. Mason is her son, my cousin who was sixteen. Mason is the best big cousin to the boys, and his presence was immediately comforting for them. We all stayed up late that night, but even when we went to bed, none of us slept. Our state of shock, disbelief, and heartache took over.

Josh, Jason, and I snuggled up in Mike's and my bed. My two brokenhearted boys slept on either side of me for months. None of us wanted to be alone, and I know it was comforting for them to sleep where their dad had slept. That night, along with just about every evening after, I lay there in the middle of my boys who were sound asleep and silently sobbed. I perfected the silent cry so I would never wake them. Every night I wished I wouldn't wake up the next morning. That is how broken I was.

I lay there pondering, *God, why Mike? Why did You have to take him?* I do not know why Mike had to die that night. I will never understand. I will never think it is fair that he was taken way too soon from us. I can only trust God and His plan. I can only believe exactly what I told my precious boys on that evening. Heaven must have needed a hero, and my husband was the strongest, bravest man who God chose to fulfill the job.

Chapter 6

---⬖---

Police Wife to Police Widow

At the time, we didn't realize how young we were. Twenty-one-year-old newlyweds excited to not only begin our lives together, but our careers as well. We were happy in our little two-bedroom apartment in Santa Clara, adjusting to life together as a married couple. My favorite part about that time was not having to say goodbye to him at the end of the day.

Everything was new, exciting, and my little dream of being a wife and taking care of my husband had come true. It was the ultimate game of house, and I loved everything about cooking him dinner after our long days, decorating our little apartment kitchen in a sunflower theme and even doing his laundry. Even though he hated my smelly candles and decorative throw pillows, at only twenty-one, we felt like we had waited so long for this moment in our lives together. Dating since we were eighteen and waiting to graduate college before we got married, it was finally here, and we were loving every second.

We had our daily routines down. We would both head out in the mornings, me to the elementary school where I was teaching third grade and Mike to the police department for another grueling day in the police academy. No texting then and definitely no phone communication with him during his days in the academy. When we both got home at the end of the day, we had so much to tell each other. I loved hearing the stories of what he got yelled at for that day by his TAC Officer or how he almost crapped his pants the day he realized during inspection that he had accidentally left his gun at home.

We would come home and spend our evenings on the couch together in our tiny living room watching TV while I graded papers and he shined his boots and duty belt. I would test him on the ten codes and the duty manual. I washed his uniform, and he would iron it. We repeated our routine together night after night. So young, so in love, and so naïve about what the future held.

I knew his days were stressful in the academy. I tried my best to make our time at home together as stress-free as I could. One mistake made in police academy and it could all be over, yet he always handled himself so well. Always calm, collected, and looking forward to the next day's challenge. He and I both made amazing friendships with his academy mates, as well as their spouses. Many of those exact friends were with me the night he was killed, and to this day they have never left my side or stopped supporting me and my sons. Police families have a special bond. We are all tightknit and support each other through all the stages of life and careers with the unspoken realization that any of us could face the tragedy of our officer never coming home.

While Mike was going through the police academy, I was extremely fortunate to be able to go through an academy of my own. It was called Family Academy. It was organized by the chaplains of the police department. My favorite night during Family Academy was when three police wives came and spoke. All three women had different perspectives on being law enforcement spouses. One had only been a couple years in with the perspective of being a new police wife and was more relatable to me at that time. Another was married to a sergeant with the perspective I was hoping to experience in the next ten-plus years. The last, whose husband had already retired, was who I was looking forward to being once Mike had finished his career in law enforcement.

In December 2005, Mike graduated from the San Jose Police Academy. Three months pregnant with our first son, I pinned his police badge on his uniform at his graduation. I was so proud of him. If the police academy was not stressful enough, he was about to enter FTO, which was field training with another experienced officer. Four weeks on day shift, four weeks on swing shift, and four weeks on midnights, each with a different training officer. Then, another two weeks back with the original field-training officer, all with your every move analyzed and documented. This was followed by up to a year of probation, evaluations, testing daily, and an oral exam in front of the oral board at the ten-month mark. It was quite the process for both of us, but of course, Mike passed with flying colors because that is who he was: hardworking, smart, and one damn good police officer.

I was pregnant with Josh throughout Mike's weeks in FTO. I continued to have pregnancy scares and went into early labor multiple times. There were few times when Mike and his FTO had to meet me in full uniform at the hospital just to find out it was another false labor. The morning of May 30, 2006, I was in labor yet again. He was not too thrilled with me when I told him it was time to go back to the hospital. Luckily, this was the real thing, and by 3:30 p.m., over a month earlier than anticipated, we welcomed our tiny five-pound baby boy, Joshua Alec, into the world. I had never seen Mike prouder than I did on that day.

He was able to take six weeks off with me after we had Josh. Two twenty-three-year-old first-time parents who were clueless on how to take care of our new baby boy, but we did it. We learned together. Really, the two of us grew up together. Mike told me early on he wanted two sons. He would joke and say he didn't make girls, only boys. He was right because when Josh was sixteen months old, we found out I was pregnant again.

I remember lying down with Mike at my side holding my hand while patiently waiting for the sonographer to give us the news, boy or girl. Mike was confident as ever that we were having another boy. He beamed with pride when she called out, "It's a boy!" I cried, but not happy tears. I really wanted a daughter, and when I heard it was another boy, I cried.

Once we got back in our car, I couldn't even call my mom to tell her we were having another boy. With no hesitation, Mike called both our parents and proudly told them the good news. He teased me for years to come about how I cried when we found out Jason was a boy. He teased Jason too. I wouldn't change that day for the world. His dream of having two boys became a reality not only on that day, but more so on May 28, 2008, when we welcomed another early, tiny baby boy into the world, Jason Daniel. Our family was complete.

As the years went by, we still spent many of our nights home when he was off work because he typically worked night shifts. We would sit on the couch together as I graded papers and he shined his boots, but now with two little boys playing all around us in our living room at the same time. We were always told how difficult it is for law enforcement families and especially for police wives. The divorce rate was high. We knew divorce was not an option for us, so we did everything possible to make Mike's love of his career work into our family.

I held close the words of advice from the three police wives who spoke in Family Academy as I journeyed through being a police wife myself. Proud to be a police wife, yes. Loved seeing my man in uniform, yes. Easy being a police wife, no. His schedule sucked. His days off hardly ever matched up with mine. We had to plan our lives in six-month increments due to shift changes, and I never knew what the new shift change would entail. Often, he would come home quiet or even grumpy. I quickly learned that meant something scary happened, and he needed some space, some time to process. The boys and I would attend family functions without him. I attended parties and weddings by myself. He missed holidays, birthdays, and anniversaries all due to a work schedule he had no control over. I would often complain that I was a single mom.

Looking back, I had it made. I wish I would have seen that then. I wish I wouldn't have complained to him. What I wouldn't give to have him back working some crappy shift while I attended a friend's party without him. To have him miss a birthday but still come home the next morning. To be stressed out and tired from another long day of no help with the kids because he was sleeping through the day and working a night shift. To be frustrated that he got a time-off request denied because they were short-staffed in the motors unit. Because all of that would mean he was still here with us.

Over the years, I started to get the hang of being a police wife. I got used to the crappy schedule and the long days of what I considered at the time as being a single mom. That term took on a whole new meaning when I did indeed become a true single mom with no husband coming home after a long night shift. I got used to it all because that was all I knew. I didn't know the life of a husband working an eight-to-five job or having the same days off as me. This was our life. Our different, nonconventional, ships-in-the-night, "single parent," perfect-to-me life. Perfect because throughout all the hardships, struggle, and stress that comes with being a police family, there was more love and commitment to outweigh any of those other things times twenty.

Eventually, I was given the opportunity to be that young police wife with only about eight to ten years of experience when I was asked to be on the other end of that Family Academy. I was asked to speak with each academy class and talk to their families and spouses about what it was like to be married to a police officer and offer any advice I may have, not knowing at the time that I would soon never be a police wife again, only a police widow. Unfortunately, for those family members who now sit in the seats at the family academies, I am their worst nightmare.

One of the best pieces of advice we were given when Mike started the police academy was to always live off your base pay and never rely on overtime to pay your bills. This stuck with Mike to the very end. I can never thank the person enough who shared that advice with us. During Mike's eleven years as a police officer, he only took overtime shifts when it was mandatory. All his days off were always one hundred percent devoted to our boys and me. We went on so many family adventures of camping, fishing, dirt-bike riding, and even just days spent at home together, something I will forever be grateful we had.

The times we spent as a family together are now the memories our sons hold so dear to their hearts. The quality time Mike spent with us rather than working overtime shifts on his days off is priceless. Even though we often could have used extra income, the time Josh and Jason got to spend with their dad in their short eight and ten years with him are filled with more adventures and memories than some people will have in a lifetime.

Our two favorite places to adventure together as a family were Hollister Hills and Lake Alpine. In the summers Mike typically had three mid-weekdays in a row off. Every single week we would head out on his days off to one of these places, not to mention any break or holiday we could get away for as well. For our Hollister Hills trips, he would load up all four of our dirt bikes. We would spend our days riding around the trails and tracks together and our nights by the fire under the stars. On our Alpine Lake trips, he would load up the kayak and fishing poles. We would spend our days on the lake fishing and our nights grilling the fish on the fire under the stars.

Family first. Time is the best investment in your children's lives. Opportunities to make more money may always be there but loved ones won't. These could all be mottos to describe the way Mike lived. This was beyond evident at his memorial service when our sons picked exactly what they wanted to display on that huge stage at SAP Center in San Jose to represent their dad. The same arena that he had taken them to watch the San Jose Sharks play hockey or the Harlem Globetrotters play basketball. It now became an arena they themselves chose how and what to display to honor their dad.

On the huge stage they chose to have his dirt bike, his kayak with fishing poles, a basketball hoop with a basketball, his guitars, and sports jerseys. Our sons never mentioned having anything police related, besides his police motorcycle, on the stage. The stage of a fallen officer memorial service. Why? Because to them and to me, he was not Officer Michael J. Katherman. To them, he was Dad. He was the one who taught them how to ride their dirt bikes, tie fishing knots, shoot hoops, and to love Jesus. To me, he was my husband, my college sweetheart, my first love, my protector, provider, my best friend. Out of all the decisions we had to make the week following the day he was killed, choosing which items to display to show a little more of Mike's personality as a man and not a cop was easy. It was everything he loved to do with the three of us.

Chapter 7

My Best Act Yet

The days leading up to the memorial service were a blur. Every moment felt like an out-of-body experience. It was as if I were living someone else's life or in a terrible dream I tried so hard to wake myself from. I was in denial and almost convinced myself at times that Mike was just away at work or on a camping trip with his friends. I would daydream at any moment we would hear the roar of his police motorcycle driving down our street, garage door opening, our dog Roxy barking in excitement for her daddy to be home, hearing his boots thud through the house to come find me, kiss me hello, and ask how my day was. That moment was never going to happen again.

The morning after Mike's death, floods of people showed up beginning early in the morning, and the revolving door never closed for days. I never had a moment to fall apart or even realize what was happening because I was too busy hosting person after person who came to our house to pay their respects. As overwhelming as it was, every single person meant well, and I am thankful for their incredible support. At one point in the day, I remember having to take chairs outside on the front lawn in order to have a meeting with representatives from the police department on what was to happen next. There were too many people inside the house.

Over the next six days, I had to attend meeting after meeting, open my home to visitor after visitor, make one important decision after another. I had to be professional, put together. The graceful wife of the fallen officer. On the inside I was absolutely dying. I had gone days without eating or sleeping. Any task I tried to do took me forever to complete. I remember how trying to shower and get myself ready each morning would take me hours. Just putting on my mascara would take minutes. It was as if I were in slow motion. The emotional pain I was feeling was also physical. I couldn't focus, see straight, breathe well, or really function at all.

There was one thing the boys and I found most comforting. There were officers taking watch outside of our house, around the clock. They made sure the boys and I were safe, sheltered from media or unwanted visitors, and cared for. These men and women took shifts for over two weeks. They gave us such comfort and peace. Some of the officers I had never met before, and many of them were close friends. All of them were working extra hours over and above their normal shifts, leaving their own families, all to make sure their fellow brother's family was taken care of.

During that week, along with planning the perfect memorial to honor Mike, there were so many other decisions to be made. Decisions that no thirty-three-year-old wife should have to make. One of the earliest and hardest for me was deciding if I was going to donate Mike's organs. The thought never even crossed my mind until late in the evening on the night he was killed I got a phone call from the hospital. A woman on the other end was a representative from the hospital who called and casually asked if I would like to donate my dead husband's organs. I remember answering the phone in the hallway of our house. As soon as she asked me that question, I walked into the boys' room, shut the bedroom door, and collapsed on the bottom bunk.

I had no clue what to do. I had no clue what that would even entail if I said yes. There was no way I could decide in a matter of a five-minute phone call. I told the woman I didn't know what to do. She made it clear that my decision was time sensitive, and she would call me back first thing in the morning. After I hung up with her, I called Mike's parents. I asked them what I should do. They calmly told me they would support whatever decision I made. I wrestled with what to do all night. I will still never be content with the decision I made. I wish Mike and I would have talked about this when he was alive. I wish I knew what he would have wanted.

The lady from the hospital called back first thing the next morning, just like she said she would. There was no stalling or procrastinating a decision like this one. I couldn't bear to think of anyone cutting Mike and dismantling him, let alone touching him. I told the lady no. She stressed to me that many lives could be saved by his. He had valuable parts that were needed. I still said no.

To this day, I feel selfish. I do not have many regrets from all the unthinkable decisions I had to make so quickly during that first week, but this one will forever linger in my mind and haunt my conscience. Was I selfish? Did I do what Mike would have wanted? All I know is, I was in utter shock and still believed he was not dead and coming home. If I would have let them take parts from him, it would have confirmed the horrible dream I was in. I will never know if I made the right choice. I will always wonder how many lives he could have saved. As a side note, I tell you now, talk to your loved ones about this. Tell them your wishes and listen to theirs. It will save a lot of heartache if you do.

Next, I had to decide quickly where Mike would be buried. A second ceremony at the burial site was to take place after the memorial service. This was also something he and I never talked about. Who does when they are as young as us? I didn't know where the hell I was supposed to "lay my husband to rest." What I did know is I just wanted him home to rest with me in our bed, not alone in the ground.

It had to be close to where we lived so the boys and I could go there anytime, and it had to be a place Mike would love. One of the mornings that week, Derek picked me up. He had now become one of my family-liaison officers. He drove me to the local cemetery. I didn't drive myself anywhere for over a month, maybe even longer. Thank the Lord for my two liaison officers, Derek and Anthony. They did more for me than I will ever realize or know, and they still do so much for us. They were grieving the loss of their buddy, too, but as always, they stayed so strong for the boys and me.

Derek and I met Anthony at the cemetery, along with the director of the funeral home. We followed her around from one empty plot to another. I had to keep it together that day and stay focused on the task at hand, but I was mad. I was mad at Mike. Why did he leave me to make all these crappy decisions on my own? We made all our decisions together. On that day I was deciding where the boys and I were going to go for the rest of our lives to "visit" him.

It was a beautiful summer day. A day that should have been spent with me, Mike, and the boys in the outdoors on a camping trip or at Hollister Hills riding dirt bikes for the day. Instead, I walked from one section of the cemetery to the other. I quickly said no to the first two spots. They were not right. Then we walked to the complete opposite side of the cemetery. There was a beautiful tree shading the grass. It was quiet. It felt like I was out in the mountains somewhere. It smelled like camping. That was it.

When I saw how much shade the grass area got, I knew. Mike was a huge wuss in the sun. But this was not what solidified my decision. In front of Mike would be another local hero, a marine killed while deployed. Next to Mike would be two more veterans. This was the heroes spot of the cemetery. At least this is what I told my boys when I got home. This was where their dad belonged. With all the heroes.

One more big decision had been made with a million more to go. All decisions that were changing our lives forever. Each requiring me to make quickly. I wrestled with each one, never knowing if I was making the right choice. Everything seemed so final and painful. A stab to the heart every time I signed my name, walked into another meeting, or tried to stay clear of media who felt the need to follow our every move.

The media presence the night I was taken to the hospital to see Mike was nothing compared to the day he was escorted from the coroner to the funeral home. And again, on the day he was taken from the funeral home to the memorial service. As a little girl, I would dream of being on television or in the movies. I enjoyed performing in front of people whether it be singing, dancing, cheerleading, or putting on plays for my family with my cousins when we were younger. Now I was displayed on one of the biggest platforms there was—local, state, and national news. Mine and my husband's names and pictures were all over social media and the internet. Personal pictures were taken off our social media pages without my permission and blasted on the nightly news. I was on television all right, playing the biggest acting role of my life. Acting the part of the poised, held-together, strong widow of fallen Officer Michael J. Katherman. I was awful at it, and I hated every second.

The day Mike was transported from the coroner's office to the funeral home, my family and I were picked up from our house in a small, black, luxury bus with black-tinted windows. We were driven from our house in Hollister to San Jose. As we neared the coroner's office, citizens lined the streets and uniformed officers stood in perfect formation. Many of the citizens stood at attention, held signs and flags while they stared at the black bus driving the fallen officer's family. Once we arrived, we sat and waited in the bus for people to clear the road and for the media presence, which was everywhere, to disperse.

I requested for my boys and I not to be filmed, photographed, or asked to be interviewed. The media never listened. I can still pull up pictures online of me with my arms wrapped around Jason and my mom's wrapped around Josh as we stood and watched our hero being carried by his fellow motors officers in his flag-draped casket from the back door of the coroner's office into the hearse. Even behind closed gates, the media still captured their shots via helicopters.

We followed behind my husband's body as we were escorted in our little black bus by the motorcade to his next destination, which was the funeral home. Dozens of police motorcycles, police cars, and media vans led us there. More people lined the streets to pay their respects. I remember sitting in the back seats of that little bus next to my dad. He held my hand as I stared out the window. I had only ever seen my dad cry twice in my life. Once when my little sister got sick as a baby and was in the hospital. I was five years old. The second time was on Mike's and my wedding day. On this day, sitting next to his brokenhearted little girl in the back of a small black bus following his dead son-in-law, he cried.

Once we arrived at the back entrance of the funeral home, I asked to stay in the bus while they transported Mike's body from the hearse to inside the building. While everyone else stood outside to respectfully watch, as officers stood at attention, as media still tried to creep their way in, I sat in the bus not wanting to see any of it. I couldn't bear seeing that flag-draped casket anymore. As much as I wanted to go home, curl up in my bed and sob, my fallen-officer-widow responsibilities were far from over that day.

Once I got the okay that he was out of sight, it was time for me to go inside for yet another meeting and more decisions to make. My mom and dad, Mike's parents, my aunt, and grandparents were with me. They all sat in a side room entertaining Josh and Jason while I went into an adjacent room—a large room full of caskets. I slowly walked circles around that room. Shopping was one of my favorite hobbies, but shopping for my husband's casket was the worst shopping trip I will ever make. The current one he was in was a loaner. I had to pick the final one he would be in for his service and burial. As my boys played with my family in one room, my husband lay dead in another. I was being an actress once again attempting to calmly and wisely make a decision I had no idea how to make.

I do not remember what color I ended up choosing. I do

know his police badge was etched into the top. I remember attempting to pick the four accessories to be attached to each corner. I flipped through the catalog pages, clueless on what to choose. I finally decided to take the catalog to my boys in the next room and let them choose. Another decision I wrestled with. What kind of mom was I to defer a decision like that to my children? *Hey, boys, do you want to pick some decorations for the huge box your dad's body is going to get buried in?*

They looked through the options and made deciding look easy. They chose a fish jumping out of the water for their dad and their love of fishing, a basketball net with a basketball in it for them and their dad's favorite sport, a police badge, and a US Navy emblem to represent their Uncle Nate, Mike's brother. Regardless of forgetting the color, I do remember the casket being beautiful. No one really saw every detail the boys and I picked out on that day's shopping trip, though, because the casket was always covered in a flag.

Once that decision was made, I left the eerie casket-filled room and was brought into a large office where I was supposed to plan my husband's memorial service. I sat with the command staff from the police department, my liaison officers, and funeral directors listening to a routine schedule of how a fallen police officer service was to be done. As I respectfully sat and listened, I got out my notepad full of my plans I had written down. In my mind, this was not going to be just another fallen officer's memorial service where Mike's name would be inserted in the blank and proper routine and protocol would be followed to appease all those in attendance and watching on TV. Honoring Mike's wishes of not inviting the mayor was also a must. I was going to make certain this would be the memorial service of not just Officer Katherman, but of Mike: husband, dad, son, brother, friend, and most importantly, man of God.

Mike had lived for thirty-four years. He was a police offi-cer for only eleven of those. I wanted his service to honor him as the overall man he was, not just the cop. I was determined we wouldn't follow the outline printed for each fallen officer memorial. We were going to follow the outline I created specif-ically for my husband, and more importantly, an outline that would honor God and be a witness to the thousands who were going to be in attendance. A witness of what it truly looked like to live a Christ-centered life and for all to know that Mike was now safe in the arms of our Heavenly Father.

Chapter 8

⚜

From City Slicker to Country Boy

I grew up a country girl and lived on a ranch much of my childhood in the small town of Gardnerville, Nevada. I married a city boy, born and raised in San Jose, California. Our worlds growing up couldn't have been more opposite of each other. I like to joke and say I turned my city boy into a country boy.

During spring break of our freshman year in college, I took Mike home with me to Gardnerville for the first time. Mike often said the only reason he continued to date me for so long was because he loved where my parents lived. For the first time in his life, my city boy was able to four wheel his Jeep, shoot guns off the back porch, ride dirt bikes, hike, and even discover old mines, all on the eighty-eight acres where my parents lived. From that moment on, all things country became something he loved. Maybe even a little more than me.

Our little family was growing and soon it was time for the next phase in our lives—home ownership. We were excited to move from the busy, crowded city of Santa Clara to the sweet little slow-paced town of Hollister. We were both hooked. I finally felt more at home, and Mike enjoyed his first time living outside the city limits. We didn't mind the commute into San Jose for work, which on a good day was an hour each way, sometimes more in traffic. Once we were home, it felt like we were away from everything and everyone.

After about five years, we sold our first home in Hollister and moved into our second about thirty minutes away in Gilroy. Unfortunately, with the city of San Jose's budget cuts, which hit the police department pretty hard, we didn't have a choice but to sell and move. Gilroy was fine, but all too soon, we were itching to move back to Hollister, but this time with land.

Our current house in Gilroy was busting at the seams with toys. I do not mean the boys' toys. I mean Daddy's toys. We were country folks living in a three-bedroom house with a two-car garage. Mike's garage and shed in the backyard were precisely organized to fit all his manly toys. Toys that belonged on property in a huge garage, shop, or barn. Having all those were a dream for him.

We made a goal to take a few years and save as much money as we could. We were determined to save enough for a down payment on a house with land. In fact, we decided we were not going to buy another home unless it had land. We were even willing to purchase a fixer-upper or downsize to a smaller home as long as it had some type of acreage.

During the school year, Mike's days off from work always landed in the middle of the week when I was teaching and the boys were in school. Most days Mike would either get together with some of his buddies and go dirt-bike riding or hop on his street motorcycle and go for a long drive. It was a way for him to decompress after a stressful week at work on the streets of San Jose. He was always back at home when the boys and I got home from school. Oftentimes he would pick up the boys from school so I could get some extra work done in my classroom. Rarely did he take them home to do homework though. Most days they would hop in the Jeep with the top off to go get some ice cream.

One day Mike was driving the back roads of Hollister on his motorcycle and came across a lone street called Lovers Lane. On Lovers Lane there was a run-down old house for sale on some land. It didn't just have a large garage; it had the garage attached to the house and also a three-car garage attached to the back of a barn, along with two smaller rooms off each side of the barn, which could be little workshops. Mike's dream.

I remember when Mike called me during my lunch break. The excitement in his voice told me he found something great. He quickly called our realtors, John and Jennifer. John met Mike at the house on Lovers Lane, all while I was still at school teaching. The repairs and upgrades needed on the house were extensive. If we purchased it, we would be in over our heads with repairs, not to mention a timeline of years to complete. But there was land, there was room for all of Mike's toys. He told me the house needed work, but "I can do it," and "The land will be worth it all." He couldn't wait to show me.

Another day, after the boys and I got out of school, all four of us met John and Jennifer on Lovers Lane. I was not sure what to expect, but seeing Mike's excitement about this place, I knew it had to be something special. We took country roads to get to Lovers Lane. Once we got to the long country road the home was on, it was refreshing to see spaced-out properties rather than homes smashed together in a neighborhood. We saw farmland, and horses and quiet were the sounds we heard along the road.

We pulled up onto the long, cracked asphalt driveway to the side of the house. The house itself was an eyesore and immediately screamed "fixer-upper" before we even stepped inside. But the barn! The barn sat off to the left side of the property behind the house and was beautiful. Big, red, sliding double doors on the front with a large hay loft on top. The barn sold the house. The acre of grass the barn sat on was a bonus.

We walked in the side door of the house onto a cement slab floor of what was the previous owners' fruit room. They kept all the fruit they picked from the various fruit trees around the property spread out on tables in this dark added-on room in order for it to ripen and be sold. To us it looked like the potential to be an awesome mudroom. Once we made our way through this addition to the house, we already had a mile-long list of needed repairs. Mike was not intimidated. Next he brought us into the main part of the house to a big empty room off the living room, and all I could say was, "Gross!"

Did he seriously want us to not only live here but spend all we had in our savings to buy this place? It was a dump—dark wood paneling; stained square ceiling tiles; linoleum floor pulling up; cracks in the walls, which allowed rodents and bugs of all kinds to get in. It was a small three-bedroom house—with the possibility to be a four-bedroom. It smelled musty and old. The house was vacant and had been for quite some time. It was hard for me to get past the visual appearance and see the vision Mike had in his head. I knew there was definitely potential in this little farmhouse, but I also knew it was going to take a lot of hard work, time, and money.

The views, the land, the barn, and the picturesque sunset sold us. I should say they sold *Mike*. I had a hard time getting over the dead bugs on the ground and the old-house smell. He would have made an offer before I even saw it. I trusted him and knew if anyone could make this house our dream home, he could. Plus, what could be better than having an address on Lovers Lane?

We scrambled to get everything we needed and put in an offer on the house. We waited impatiently to hear from John and Jennifer with news of whether our offer was accepted. We were disappointed to hear it was not. Someone else had beat us to it. We were bummed. This was the only home on land in our price range available at the time, and we didn't get it. Disappointed, we decided we would just stay put in our current house for a couple of more years, save some more, then look again.

About two months later, Mike was out on another motorcycle ride. As he cruised through the country roads in Hollister, he decided to drive down Lovers Lane and take a peek on the house to see what kind of work had been done. To his surprise, nothing. No work done, and it was still vacant. He quickly ended his ride, drove straight home, and called John. Sure enough, after doing some digging, John found out the original offer fell through, and it was back on the market.

Within hours we submitted a second offer, this time with a sappy letter explaining to the seller our plans to fix up their home that had been in their family for so many years and make it our own little dream home to raise our family in. It worked, and they accepted. Even better, the reason the original offer fell through was because there were some major issues the buyer found wrong with the house and backed out. The owner fixed them all before putting the house back on the market. It ended up being a big win for us. A couple of items were already marked off our mile-long repair list, and we didn't even have to pay for it.

The escrow process was not long, but for us, it seemed like forever. Since the home was vacant, some days we would pack up a lunch or dinner and some chairs to go have a little picnic out on the property. We were totally trespassing at the time, but we were too excited to care. We could never get inside the house, so we would walk circles around the property while the boys ran around in pure freedom, dreaming about all we were going to do to make that slice of heaven our forever home.

After signing our lives away to another mortgage, we moved from Gilroy into our fixer-upper. We got the keys, and the repairs began rather instantly. Mike and his dad started by replacing the water heater, which quickly turned into a much bigger issue and project than they thought. It was a window into the foreseeable future as to what was to come with fixing up an old, run-down house. Again, Mike was never phased. He would work on project after project during all his free time. The boys would run wild with our dog, Roxy, ride their dirt bikes, play basketball, have Nerf wars in the barn, shoot their BB guns, and explore. It was a little-boy-outdoor paradise.

Mike had big plans for our beautiful barn. All his toys were already parked in their precise spots in the attached three-car garage. One of the side shops on the barn was designated as his wood shop. The other housed his new riding lawn mower and all things lawn maintenance. There was no way he was going to pay a gardener to take care of *his* property. His parents bought him the riding lawn mower as a housewarming gift, and it sure got its use each week. Even the boys mowed the field, riding happily with their dad.

The inside of the barn was set up as a huge game room. It had a pool table, foosball table, and dart board. The next project in the barn was Mike's huge bar he was going to build. Boy, was that space going to be amazing! The top part of the barn, the hay loft, was filled with the boys' board games, Legos, and Nerf guns. Mike had plans to eventually turn that area into a theater for the kids. Our dream to-do list was long, but amazing. Knowing it would be our forever home, we were going to take our time and go all out as we worked to create our own little haven for our family away from it all.

Small and large repairs were happening daily. The big-ticket items were all being marked off our list. New roof, re-piping the house, pulling out the old, broken wall heaters and having central air and heat installed. We were making great progress, but nothing cosmetic was being done, which was hard for this interior decorating-loving girl. I was ready to "Joanna Gaines" the house, and we were far from ready for that.

Being the attentive husband he was, Mike quickly noticed how impatient I was getting. He decided to start demoing the hallway bathroom so I could have my own project. It was also the boys' bathroom, and it was pink. No boys of his were going to have a pink bathroom, so it worked to my advantage.

The demolition of the bathroom took longer than it should have but for an exceptionally good reason. Mike let the boys help him. He showed them which tool to use, its name, and how to use it, and then let them go to town. What he could have done in a day while we were all at school took almost a week. This is how Mike did everything. He took the time to teach the boys along the way. I believe this is why our oldest son, Josh, is so handy. At nine, he was old enough to remember what his dad taught him.

As the demolition in the bathroom continued, Mike placed anything that could be salvaged into the spare bedroom. Talk about an eyesore. A toilet sat there for all to see, along with tools, pipes, paint, insulation, and who knows what else. It became the catchall room for all-things-bathroom remodel related.

Once Mike and the boys were done with the demolition, Mike decided he would let someone else take over the tile work. We picked out the perfect farmhouse look complete with subway tiles, hexagon-shaped floor tiles, and wainscoting on the bottom half of the walls. I knew I wanted gray color for the walls. Mike must have put up more than ten samples for me. My indecisive self couldn't decide on which shade, so I let him pick, and the winner was called Stone Fireplace. Stone Fireplace was so perfect that I ended up using it throughout the whole house.

As the school year ended, summer was just around the corner. Even though we had camping trips planned on most of Mike's days off, he still somehow managed to make time to work on the house. I was looking forward to the tile work being completed so Mike could finish remodeling the bathroom. This would mean it would be my turn to make it look pretty.

The bathroom did end up looking beautiful. A farm-house-style that would have made Joanna Gaines proud. Unfortunately, it took months to complete, and it was not completed by Mike. The day the tile crew was finishing their work on the bathroom was the day Mike was killed. The day my house was filled with police command staff, city officials, and our best friends who had come to tell me the devastating news,

I still had a toilet sitting in the spare bedroom. Mike's tools were spread throughout the house, and his paint-sample cans were piled high in the corner.

Our big dreams and our big plans had only just begun. They all came to an abrupt halt in the summer of June 2016. The bathroom sat unfinished for weeks. As the visitors filed in and out of my house day after day and week after week, Mike's unfinished project stood still. The toilet never moved. His tools never moved. Eventually, our dads worked together to finish what Mike had started.

Eventually, word got out to the community about the plans Mike had for our dream farmhouse. This small renovation Mike had begun started something I could have never done on my own.

Chapter 9

Walking through Curtains

The morning of the memorial service arrived. My house was filled with family, each of us quietly getting ready for the long day ahead. Just like it had been for me each morning since Mike's death, it took me a long time to get myself ready. I often stopped and braced myself on the bathroom sink in between my cries. At one point I realized I had no waterproof mascara and texted my aunt Paulett, asking her to bring me some. I had to stop and pause between each application of makeup, each curl of my hair, and as I got dressed. It took a long time. My mom brought me a plain bagel so I would have something in my stomach. I ate one bite and left the rest on the bathroom counter. Even after seven days, I still couldn't stomach anything.

My journal entry reflecting back on that morning really said it all:

As I got ready in the morning, I felt like I wasn't in my own body or even my own life. It took me so long to get ready. Not just that day, but I was like that for a really long time. I couldn't focus long enough to get through blow drying my hair in one sitting or applying my makeup. It just took too much effort and strength that I didn't have.

I had tried on multiple different outfits the night before. Nothing fit, I had already lost so much weight. I really didn't want to wear black. I settled on a navy blue dress I borrowed from Paulett. I knew I would be on my feet all day, so I decided on comfortable flats rather than heels. My close police-wife girlfriends gifted me a necklace that replicated Mike's police badge. I wore it proudly around my neck.

I do not know who got my boys ready that morning, but I assume it was my mom. They looked so handsome. Morgan had taken them earlier in the week to get fitted for suits, something I would have never even thought to do. I tried my best to prepare them as to what was going to come on this day. It was going to be a long day for all of us. I do not think I really knew what to expect myself.

The black cars arrived to escort us, as well as the whole motors unit from the police department. Our long driveway was lined with police motorcycles. Each officer got off his motorcycle and walked in their long, shined, black boots across the grass in silence. They each took off their helmet to give me a hug. I felt a mixture of comfort and heartache. Comfort that all of Mike's teammates were there to help guide, protect, and get us through this terrible day, yet heartache that I would never see my husband in complete motors uniform like they were ever again.

We gathered around each other, took some deeps breaths, and my dad prayed for this big day we were all about to face. It took a while before my family loaded into the black cars and the guys got back on their bikes. I do not think any of us wanted to face the reality of what lay ahead. The motorcycles led the way in perfect formation as we followed behind Derek in his police car. Anthony drove me, Josh, Jason, and my parents in a blacked-out suburban. I was relieved that no one could see inside, yet it was obvious who we were.

As we left our house and started down our country road, I saw neighbors outside their houses waving to us under their flags raised at half-mast. Some held hands over their hearts to signal their support to us. As we made our way out of Hollister and onto Highway 101 toward San Jose, every single overpass for the next thirty miles was lined with fire trucks, fireman in uniform standing at attention, citizens standing at attention, American flags—both gigantic and small—hanging off the side, handmade signs waved above heads.

Once we got off the freeway and onto the side streets that led us to our first stop of the day, the funeral home, the streets were lined with people. There were boys in their Boy Scout uniforms standing at attention, little girls waving their handmade glittery RIP Officer Katherman signs, flags being waved, more people paying their respects to the city's hero, our hero. Media vans and press lined the sidewalks in front of the mortuary. We waited for the all-clear sign before we were able to exit the vehicle and go into the building.

We entered the funeral home where Mike was waiting for me. I say me, because you better believe after not getting enough time with him seven days earlier, I sure as hell was going to be the first to be with him and spend as much time as I wanted. We were ushered inside, and the foyer was lined with giant poster-sized pictures of our family on easels. There was a table with a book to sign, which was filled with signatures. There was also a giant picture of Mike in uniform for people to sign. I didn't realize how many people came to pay their respects during visiting hours that week until I saw all those names.

I saw yet another curtain separating me from him, just like at the hospital. I remember telling my mom I could do this by myself. I took a deep breath and walked down that center aisle of the little chapel inside the funeral home to my husband. But, boy, was this different than walking down the aisle of a beautiful chapel to him twelve years prior. This time he was not standing at the end looking handsome in his suit and tie. He was lying in the casket the boys and I designed, etched beautifully with his badge, looking dead in his uniform and tie. He was in complete police uniform down to the shined boots. The same uniform I had to take out of our closet and hand over days prior for my dead husband to be buried in. I pulled up a chair, sat beside him, held his hand, and just sobbed. It was a good thing Paulett brought me that waterproof mascara. It just didn't seem real. *Get up! Get up and take me home!* I screamed silently.

I am quite sure my mom kept looking through the curtain down that long aisle to check on me because at one point, my dad came in. My dad held me as I sobbed. He stayed so strong when I knew it was breaking his heart to see his little girl like this. The whirlwind of the week hit me in the face at that very moment. This moment was the last time I would ever see my husband face to face on this earth.

I knew I needed to get myself together and give the boys the option to see their dad. I went to the back room where my family was keeping them entertained. I prepared them a little for what they were going to see and walked with them down the aisle. They looked at their daddy in that same uniform they last said goodbye to and hugged him in. They both stood far away until I grabbed their hands, telling them it was okay to get closer and guided them to stand in front of the casket. Of course, my silly Jason teased his dad for wearing makeup. At one point, I touched Mike's face and his caked-on makeup smudged on his nose. It made us all giggle through our tears.

The drive to the funeral home was quiet with mixed emotions of the worst pain and sadness you can ever experience, along with so much pride and honor to be Officer Katherman's wife. Once we arrived, it was my last time to say goodbye to Mike. It was the last time I was able to hold his hand, kiss his face, and physically be with him. I talked to him like he was alive and heard my every word. I told him I wish he could see how much makeup he had on because he would have hated it. He hated makeup and loved when I didn't wear any. I would never wear makeup again if it would mean him being back with me.

Josh was quieter, almost a little afraid. I cannot imagine what was going through their innocent eight- and ten-year-old minds in that moment. I will always wonder if I made the right choice of letting them see their dad like that. Will it be a memory and moment they will one day thank me for allowing them to have, or will it forever haunt them? The boys didn't stay long. They walked in, looked at their dad, and walked out.

But that was okay. I took them back to the room, kissed them both, and immediately went back to Mike.

Yet again I didn't have much time. I needed to let other family members and friends have their time, but I didn't want to leave him. I didn't want to face what was to come that day. Once I finally left him, though never wanting to, we got back into our escorted car and left for the memorial service. Media vans were still parked out front. People lined the streets all the way to the venue. Hundreds of motors officers on their motorcycles, from all over the country, served as escorts for their brother in blue and his family. From our car window, we saw no end in sight of motorcycles in front and behind us. Josh's and Jason's eyes were glued to the windows. It was an amazing sight to see.

The service took place at the SAP Center in San Jose. This was the arena that housed the same venue that held the biggest music names and their concerts. Once a happy place for an evening out as a family was transformed into a tear-stained-tribute location for Officer Michael J. Katherman.

A couple of blocks away, we began to creep slower and slower ahead. We turned a corner to see the big SAP building and the street lined with motorcycles and motors officers standing at attention saluting Mike, who was in the hearse in front of us. I remember slowly driving by, staring at the different patches on uniforms and saying out loud where these men and women had traveled from. New Jersey PD, New York PD, Washington, Nevada, agencies all over California—it was like every agency in the nation had sent representatives from their department to honor my husband. As we crossed the intersection in front of the SAP Center, I saw his picture on the giant marquee. We drove under the huge, hanging American flag held by ladders extended from fire trucks and swaying beautifully in the wind.

Crossing the intersection lined with rows and rows deep of people standing still and in silence watching as we drove by, we entered the sea of uniform personnel from San Jose Police Department. Surrounding agencies had sent officers to patrol the streets so every single San Jose police officer, dispatcher, reserve, and recruit could be in attendance. Over a thousand men and women stood shoulder to shoulder in uniform, perfectly still and silent at attention as we continued to slowly follow the car that held my husband's body. It was a scene of pure respect, honor, and love for not only Mike but us as well—the family of the fallen officer following in the unmarked car with blacked-out windows.

As we drove through the side gates behind the building, we were hidden away from all the hype going on outside. A couple of San Jose officers were waiting to direct us to the room we would wait in until the ceremony began. It was nice to see a few familiar faces, and their embraces were comforting. If I was scared not knowing what to expect, I cannot imagine how my boys were feeling. I kept them close and pointed out how we were entering the building the same way the hockey players do.

A side room was all set up for us. There was food, drinks, and lots of tissues. The essentials. I tried to get the boys to eat a snack because I knew it would be a long time before they would have a chance to eat again. We waited in the room as the SAP arena started to fill with thousands of people I didn't know. The floor seats were reserved for our family, close friends, and all San Jose police personnel. They filed into their rows in perfect formation as if they knew how to do this all too well. Unfortunately, barely a year prior, we had lost another SJPD officer in the line of duty, Officer Michael Johnson. Barely a year prior I was sitting in those same arena seats watching my husband file in to honor his brother in blue. Now they were doing the same for him.

As we waited, individuals took turns coming in and presenting the boys and me with plaques, flags, and gifts. The police chaplains came in to see how we were holding up. Even California Senator Kamala Harris made an appearance and presented the boys and me with a framed flag to honor Mike. At this point, I was exceptionally good at smiling and saying thank you while holding back my tears. After making myself and my boys use the restroom, it was time. It was time to line up behind my husband's body and slowly walk down the long hallway that led us to another curtain. Curtains in front of me seemed to define tragedy. Each curtain I walked through in those seven days held something horrific behind it. This large, black, thick curtain, which was about to be opened by the white-gloved hands of two men in uniform, held much of the same.

I held my sons' hands tight, took a deep breath, and gave the head nod which signaled I was ready. Mike lay in his flag-covered coffin extended on a stand with wheels. The Honor Guard led the way as Mike's six pallbearers wheeled him through the opened curtain. The boys and I slowly walked behind, through the opened curtain and the same tunnel the hockey players would skate through in excitement to start a game, except we walked through to start a nightmare.

I looked up and saw the seats that layered up toward the ceiling of this circular venue filled with people standing in silence. I saw news cameras set in place all over the building. At one point, one of them got in my face as I was walking, and I wanted so badly to grab it, throw it on the ground, and stomp the living shit out of it. How I wished I would have worn heels. Being televised, I understand they wanted all angles, but come on, show a little respect and give us some space.

We walked a second long aisle. The sound of the bagpipes playing behind us will forever be a sound I hate. A former beautiful sound now represented pain. I still cringe when I hear them. With Josh and Jason on either side of me, I held my head high and proudly followed my husband down the aisle lined with officers standing at attention and my closest family and friends waiting at the end to be seated near us. We were escorted to the front row. We took our seats. Out of the thousands of people in the building, we were the first to sit down. It was almost like we were signaling to all that it was okay to begin, like how the mother of the bride signals the start of a wedding ceremony. Mike was wheeled to the front of the stage just a few feet away from us with an officer standing at attention on each side of him to take watch.

> *At the service when we walked down that center aisle with all eyes on us behind his casket, I remember thinking, "My husband is in there! Either let me in or let him out of there! Why him? Why our perfect little family?" I will always wonder why. What in the world is God's plan in all this? What is so big and so important that it needed my husband's thirty-four-year-old life to be taken in order to be accomplished?*

The stage looked beautiful. It was set up just the way the boys had requested. The music stopped, the slideshow playing on the jumbo screens hanging from the center of the arena turned off and now displayed a picture of Mike, his name, and his End of Watch Date, a date that will forever define him as a police officer. I had to take multiple deep breaths to not pass out. I realized in that moment I should have tried to eat more than a single bite of a bagel. I put my arms around Josh and Jason and held them close as we watched the tribute to their dad begin.

Various important people in our lives took the stage to talk about the amazing godly man Mike was. Many told jokes and stories which made the crowd laugh and even me smile a bit through my tears. They played a video I was not prepared to see, from Mike's police academy days. I sat with tears streaming down my face watching a flashback of my young, handsome, twenty-two-year-old husband being asked the question in an interview, "Who has been your biggest support throughout police academy?" He answered, "My wife."

He went on to explain how much of an impact I had made supporting him through every step of the long process of becoming a police officer. Just hearing his voice again, his laugh, and hearing him say my name with that big goofy smile on his face made my heart shatter once again. I had done so well to make my cries silent so no one would hear. I knew all eyes were going to be on me and my boys, but now my cries were audible for everyone to hear around me, and my shoulders shook with my sobs. There was not enough tissue to wipe my tears. I felt a few touches on my shoulder from my father-in-law and Mike's motors unit buddies, trying to show me comfort as I fell apart.

Every speaker, every salute, and every tear shed that day represented the honor and love for a man of God who loved his wife, his boys, his family, friends, department, city, and ice cream. I couldn't have been sadder and happier as to how

Mike was honored that day. My goal of glorifying God through Mike's life tribute and sharing how he will be spending eternity in heaven because of the personal relationship he had with Christ was met ten times over.

When the ceremony ended, we were escorted out of the arena the same way we entered, slowly walking behind Mike's casket and back through the black curtain. We caught our breath for a minute in the side room before making our way back outside to the escorts. Thousands left their seats in time to stand outside and pay tribute while we drove out the same way we drove in. The same officers lined the streets at attention, and the same motorcade escorted us from the SAP Center to Gilroy.

It was time for the burial.

Nothing about the week had been intimate for just my family and close friends. Everything was planned for the whole city to honor their fallen officer. To have proper closure that day, I requested that the burial ceremony be closed to the public. I only allowed our family, a few select close friends, Mike's academy class, the motors unit, and police command staff to attend. Our thirty-mile drive down Highway 101 from San Jose to Gilroy was the same as the drive earlier that morning. The same overpasses still lined with firetrucks, fireman, flags, people, and signs. Many of those people watched the ceremony live on the internet and waited for us to drive back the way we came to pay their respects once again. It was the most heartwarming display.

Once we got into our local town, the street that led us to the cemetery was lined with locals as if a parade were coming through town. I saw former students I taught and their families, families from Little League and my boys' basketball teams, families from church. Local businesses flew their flags at half-mast and put signs in their windows to honor my fallen hero. Multiple police cars and officers positioned themselves at the entrance of the cemetery as to not let anyone in who was not approved.

The police department was so kind to rent two large buses to transport our family and close friends from the arena to the cemetery to lessen the number of cars in the motorcade and to know who was to be permitted to enter. Once we slowly turned into the cemetery, we drove to the spot. The beautiful, shaded spot I had picked out for Mike a few days prior under the big tree. Just a couple of rows of chairs were set up in front of the large hole in the ground. Enough chairs for the boys and me, Mike's and my parents, and our grandparents. Most everyone else stood close all around. Finally, an intimate setting to honor my husband, not my officer. Finally, I could be the grieving widow of Mike and not the poised widow of Officer Katherman.

We took our seats in the chairs while Mike's casket was placed on a rack over the hole to be above ground, still draped in our country's flag that would soon be folded ever so precisely and handed to me. Before we began, every member of Mike's police academy made a line and hugged me one by one as I sat in the seat directly in front of Mike, all never failing to show their support to the boys and me.

Our police chaplain led the small burial ceremony. He said kind, meaningful words about my precious husband and prayed. Each corner of the flag was lifted and folded by two uniformed officers. One bent down on his knee to present it to me. The scene of a movie could have happened right then and there. I pulled the flag into my chest and hugged it tight. We laid roses on his coffin, cried, and I hugged my support system who stood all around me.

Some may not understand, many didn't on that day, but I had no desire to see Mike's body in that casket dropped into the ground and buried with dirt. I didn't want anyone to begin that process until I was long gone. It is typical for the family to stay and watch the actual burial. I just couldn't do it. I also didn't want my sons' last memory of that sad yet amazing day to be watching their dad buried in the ground. I will never know if I made the right choice for them. I just pray that my mother's intuition knew best.

Before leaving, I threw my body over his casket and sobbed. Every part of my being wanted to open it up and crawl inside with him. *Just bury me with him now,* I thought. The pain I felt was unbearable. Even though the closest people in my life were the ones surrounding me, I held back many of my tears. I worried about the scene I displayed for my children.

I kissed the coffin for the last time, hugged the last of the family and friends that were waiting to watch the burial, and got back into the car with my parents and my boys. This time just our own SJPD motors officers escorted us back home. Since Anthony was driving us, he had his police radio on him. The guys on their motorcycles were talking to Josh and Jason on the radio making them laugh. Seeing laughter instead of tears on my boys' faces as their dad's buddies made jokes and talked about ice cream is a much better memory than watching him be buried in the ground.

We finally arrived back home. I don't know what I did the rest of that day. I am sure it consisted of sitting like a zombie, not eating, crying, and not sleeping again that night, knowing the next day I had more duties to perform as the widow of fallen Officer Michael J. Katherman.

Chapter 10

High Water

Word got out to the community about the state of our farmhouse. In no time, a retired police officer formed a crew of a skilled construction team, and they worked countless hours renovating our home. The generosity of this selfless man and many others who gave of their time and skills was simply amazing.

One of the biggest tasks was knocking down a load-bearing wall that separated the kitchen and the living room. In order to have more of an open space, a huge beam needed to be placed in the ceiling for support. One weekend a crew was formed, and a plan was put into place on how to open up the floor in order to pour concrete and set pillars to hold the beams. For a couple of nights, the boys and I slept with a huge, ten-foot by four-foot hole in the floor of our living room. Only plywood covered the exposed crawl space under our house.

During one of those evenings, I had a dream. In my dream, I was standing on one side of the room looking at the huge open floor and to the other side of the room where the addition was being built. Mike stood in the new doorway, leaning with his arm against the wall. He was in his best physical form, like the Bible says we will be in heaven. He was young, so handsome, and physically fit. He looked like he did in our college days. He looked me in the eyes from across the room and simply nodded his head up and down and said, "Good job, good job." I never wanted to wake up from that dream or any dream I ever had with him in it. That night was confirmation to me that he approved of all the work these amazing men were doing to our home, and he was happy with all I was choosing to do.

By the end of the summer, the bathroom was complete, exactly the way Mike and I designed it. I was not going to change a thing. The redesigned kitchen cabinets were on order, as well as barnwood-looking plank floors. The painters had finished painting, and the walls were the perfect shade of gray Mike had originally picked. Tall baseboards, crown molding, beadboard, farmhouse-style five-plank doors with glass antique doorknobs; it was beautiful. The addition was completed too, which became Josh's new bedroom and a walk-in pantry. I had Pottery Barn furniture on order and set to be delivered in a couple of weeks. New fences had been built around the front of the property with a beautiful barndoor-looking swinging gate at the end of the driveway. New asphalt had just been poured and wrapped all the way around the barn, ending with a pad to park our toy hauler camping trailer on, exactly the way Mike had designed. Thanks to the selfless dedication of the amazing men who gave of their time and talents to bless the boys and me, our dream little farmhouse was coming together just the way we had planned. I couldn't have been more pleased with it.

In January 2017, the winter storms were intense. The wind and rain got worse day by day. Water kept getting under the big side swinging door of the barn. Every day I would go out to the barn and push the water back outside with a push broom. It was such a huge pain, and I hated that I was trying to deal with it on my own. I finally went and got sandbags and placed them all around the barn. I am not a very strong girl. I have a small build and am physically weak, so loading the sandbags into the truck on my own, unloading them, and placing them around the barn wasn't easy for me.

Each day I tried to keep the water from getting into the barn, I would get more and more mad. This was Mike's job! He would always take care of this kind of stuff. I was mad he wasn't there to handle it. He always teased me about being so weak, and I was sure he was looking down laughing, watching me struggle as I looked up and cursed him many times. My efforts helped for a couple of days. How I wish that small stressor of water getting into my barn was the least of my worries that winter.

On January 10, the boys and I went to bed together in my room. It had been barely six months since Mike had died, and both boys were still sleeping in bed with me. I didn't mind one bit; I hated being alone in our bedroom. In the middle of the night, at about 3:00 a.m., Josh woke up to use the restroom. He sat up and swung his feet down toward the ground and yelled, "Mom, Mom, there's water everywhere!" It was typical for Josh to have night terrors at that time, so that is what I thought was happening. It was dark, and I couldn't see anything. I told him it was fine and to go back to sleep. He was persistent, "No, Mom, really there is water everywhere."

Once I got myself up and my eyes adjusted, I realized, holy crap! He's right! There was water everywhere. I stepped out of the bed into about three feet of water. At this point our commotion had woken up Jason. He immediately started freaking out about his new iPad he had just gotten for Christmas. He thought he had left it on the floor in the living room, and now it was ruined. Luckily, it was safe and sound on the nightstand next to him. Yet, my iPad I used for teaching was definitely immersed in the water, and so was everything else.

I told the boys to stay in my bed while I checked things out. Not even thinking about the possibility of being electrocuted, I turned on the lights, which miraculously still worked, and trudged through the water in my socks to try and find out what the heck was going on. As I walked out of my bedroom, down the hallway, and into the living room, I continued to look up at the ceiling. I was looking for a leak in the roof. Even though my whole house was covered in three feet of water, I was not in the right frame of mind to realize it couldn't have happened as the result of a little roof leak. That is when I looked out the big new French doors in the living room that had been recently installed and saw the rushing water surrounding the back of our property. It was as if our house was an island, and we were in the middle of an ocean.

There must have been five feet of water surrounding our home. There was no way in and no way out. We were stuck. I was alone in my home with our sons completely stranded and helpless. I had no clue what to do. I was beyond scared. Like always, I knew I couldn't make a scene for my boys, so I kept my composure in order to keep them calm. I carried each one from my bed on my back through the shallow lake that was my house and had them each stand on the kitchen table.

My cell phone was plugged into the charger on the kitchen counter. I picked it up to see about fifteen missed calls from my neighbor. Our land line didn't work, and he had been trying to get ahold of me for hours now, to see if we were okay. I still cannot believe that all three of us slept through all that water rushing into our house. I called him back, and I could instantly hear the relief when he heard we were okay. He told me he had been in touch with the fire department who was on the way, so we just needed to stay put.

I had taken the boys to Disneyland about a month prior. On the flight back home, a nice man and his family noticed that our luggage tags said we lived in Hollister. He introduced himself. Once we said our names, he knew exactly who we were. It ended up that he was a firefighter for the Hollister Fire Department. He invited the boys and me to have breakfast with Santa at the fire station, so we exchanged phone numbers. There couldn't have been a more prime example of God's divine intervention. Soon my phone rang, and it was him. He stayed on the line with me for some time and walked me through all that was going to happen.

He told me we needed to stay put because it was going to be a while until we could get rescued. He was sending San Jose Fire by boat to come get the three of us out of the house to safety. In the meantime, there was nothing we could do but wait. Our dog, Roxy, was an outdoor dog, and I couldn't believe my eyes when I saw her standing on the back steps holding her head high above the water. There was nothing I could do to help her because I couldn't open the door to let her in. We had to sit and listen to her terrified whimpers. Our two cats were crying from on top of the floating fridge now turned on its side in the mudroom.

We waited for at least an hour or more before we got word that the boat was getting closer to our house. I called my parents in a panic letting them know what was going on. There was nothing they could do. They lived in another state, and the roads were all closed due to the storm. I called Morgan and Derek because they also lived in Hollister. I knew they would drop everything, even at 4 a.m., to come get us once we were taken to safety. With each phone call I made, there were no words to truly describe the terrifying situation the three of us were in.

As I looked around, there were shoes that were left out on the floor floating in the water. It got me thinking that I needed to get my head straight and figure out a plan of escape. I left the boys on the table and trudged through the water to find a dry bag on top of my bedroom closet. I filled that bag with some clothes for the three of us. I threw what I could get of mine that was hanging up because my dresser drawers were covered in water. I had to get clothes out of Josh's closet for both him and Jason because Jason's clothes were all in drawers under his bed, also covered in water. We had no dry shoes.

It never dawned on me that all of my electricity was still on, and the outlets were covered by water. I trudged through the water in my socks, back into the kitchen to be with the boys, fortunate we weren't electrocuted. At this point I was cold. My feet and legs were freezing. The water I was standing in was so cold and disgusting. Our home, along with all the others that surrounded our property, had a septic tank. The lids to the septic tanks were swept away with the flood waters. Whatever was in the cow and horse pastures were also taken with the current. I was trekking around my house in my socks through "poo water," as the boys and I fondly refer to it.

My phone rang, and it was the Hollister fireman again call-ing to let me know that San Jose Fire was getting close in their boat. Within minutes we saw a spotlight shine through the windows of our house. It was still dark outside, maybe 4:30 a.m. For the first time that night, I was not scared. I knew help had arrived, and these men were going to get us to safety. I just was not quite sure how. I heard a man's voice yell through a speaker, "If you are okay inside, flicker your lights." I splashed through the water over to the front porch light switch and flickered it to signal we were okay. The voice responded, "Just stay put. We are trying to find the best way to get you out."

We waited for what seemed like forever, yet was likely a few minutes. I continued to reassure the boys that the firemen were here, and everything was going to be okay. I knew when San Jose Fire arrived at the scene, they were sent out to our house specifically knowing who we were. The voice on the speaker caught our attention again when they yelled that they were go-ing to come through the front bedroom window by the garage. That was Josh's new room which had recently been completed. Days prior, one of Mike's buddies came and hung his TV on the wall for him. Now it was all a loss. This was the highest point in the house and where the boat could most easily access.

I heard the window open and men's voices telling us they were coming to get us and not to move. The firemen climbed from the boat, through the window, and into Josh's bedroom. They trudged through the water into the kitchen where they found the three of us sitting together on the kitchen table. They were incredibly calm, which was comforting to the boys. Seeing their familiar San Jose patches on their uniforms was comforting to me. One by one, the men had us climb onto their backs, and they carried us through the house, then helped each of us climb out the bedroom window and into the boat. One of them bravely went back in and returned with Roxy who was shivering and scared. They put Roxy into the boat with us. I was worried she was going to jump out into the lake surrounding us. Unfortunately, one of the firemen said we had to leave the cats. They did end up surviving the flood and were found roaming the property days later when the flood waters had subsided.

We were almost ready to leave the house in the boat when one of the firemen said to hold on and went back inside. We waited for him to come back out, and when he did, he looked at me and said, "I put his flag on top of the fridge." The fridge inside the house was still standing. That simple act of kindness and the fact he even noticed the flag meant so much to me. The same flag I had recently been presented with at Mike's burial was rescued and put up to higher ground. The whole time I sat in that water-filled house, I never even realized it was in harm's way. I will forever be thankful to the fireman who noticed and took action to save something he knew was so important to our family.

The boys and I, our dog Roxy, and another fireman sat in the boat as three others in full wading gear guided the boat by the light of flashlights and spotlights through the lake that used to be our long country road, Lovers Lane. One of them let the boys take turns holding the spotlight. We moved slowly as the men waded through water pushing the boat. As we floated by each home, we saw people waving their arms for help sitting on roofs or on top of their cars. The firemen would call out to them, "We will come back for you." I sat on the long bench seat of that small metal boat with each of my sons on either side of me, the small bag of clothes on my lap, and our dog at my feet. We were still in our pajamas and socks. My feet were still so cold. The men said they were going to take us to a fire truck that was waiting further down the road, and it would take us to the end of Lovers Lane. This would be higher ground, and we could either be driven to a shelter that had been set up or have someone pick us up.

Once the boat got to the fire truck, the firemen carried us on their backs in the water from the boat to the fire truck. I thanked each of them multiple times as the boys and I climbed inside. They handed Roxy to us. I sat in the back of that fire truck soaking wet holding my boys and my dog, not knowing what in the world I was going to do next. Hardly anyone even knew the terrible situation we were in at that moment until it hit the morning news. Once again I was handling something hard by myself without Mike. This time I knew he wasn't looking down laughing; I'm sure he was protecting us instead.

As we sat in that huge fire truck and began to drive away to safety, I looked out the window and back at the river, which was once our road to home. The run-down farmhouse Mike had once convinced me he could turn into a beautiful forever home was now under water. The hard work of so many in our community had just gone down in ruins. I felt such a huge sense of guilt. I felt awful that these men had given so selflessly of their time and worked so hard for months on end for it all to be destroyed. I felt like I had let Mike down, and once again, I had to sit and watch my terrified and worried children face another nightmare they didn't deserve to live through. Why, God?

The fire truck arrived at the end of Lovers Lane, and I immediately saw Derek and Morgan. They were waiting for us. We all climbed into the back of their car, and as the sun started to rise, we drove to their house in utter shock as to what had just happened. They first took us to the shelter set up in downtown Hollister. We were supposed to check in so it was documented that we were out of our residence and safe. I left the boys in the car with Derek and Morgan while I walked into the giant community hall in my soaking wet pajama pants and muddy socks. We were given blankets, fresh socks, and some snacks. Soon after, Derek and Morgan took us back to their house where they set up their guest room for us. We were now dry, safe, and with our friends who are more like family. We stayed with them for a few days while we tried to figure out what in the world had just happened.

Chapter 11

Facing the Man Who Killed My Husband

The weeks and months before the flood but following Mike's death were much of the same. Days consumed with decisions to make. Simple decisions and hard decisions, but even the simple ones were hard for me. My days were preplanned for me. There was meeting after meeting too. Meetings at the police department to sign more paperwork. Meetings with lawyers to discuss important personal matters and those involving the motorcycle accident. Meetings with different representatives from different charity groups that were holding events in Mike's honor and so much more. Then, the to-do list of phone calls to make was never-ending.

Each week Anthony would bring us boxes from the police department full of various items sent to the department for us. People from all over the country, even other countries, sent us cards and gifts. The number of items that were mailed to the police department and delivered to us from total strangers was overwhelming. I mean overwhelming in the most amazing way. I kept every single card and note sent. I saved each one in page protectors in large binders. The boys' rooms and our home in Hollister were now decorated in memorabilia made in their dad's honor. From blankets and teddy bears, to wooden flags and plaques. I documented every single gift in a notebook and made sure to send a thank you card for each one. I mailed hundreds of cards over the next months.

One night the boys and I sat with Anthony and Derek at our kitchen table to design Mike's challenge coin. A challenge coin is a small coin or medallion often collected by service members or law enforcement personnel. Mike had his own collection of about fifteen coins that he kept in a basket on his nightstand. Challenge coins originated from World War I and were developed to signify one's identity. These coins typically are earned for being in a particular unit in the police department or branch of the Army. They represent proof of membership and can be given as an award or recognition as well. They are a token of honor and respect. He religiously kept two or three coins in his pockets. He would tell me, "You never know when I can get a free meal by throwing down a challenge coin to one of my buddies." If they didn't have one on them, they were the ones who would be buying.

Anthony and Derek noticed how much the boys were into designing their dad's own personal coin. The word circulated through them to other officers, and people started sending the boys coins. At the memorial service, someone had the most brilliant idea to put tall motorcycle boots out for people to fill with their departments' challenge coins. Hundreds and hundreds of coins started to roll in from all over the world. The collection my boys now have is something that can be passed down from generation to generation. It is simply remarkable.

Being the family of a fallen officer comes with some perks. I hate to use the word "perks," but when you are in the utter state of shock and heartache, any kind of positive pick-me-up is greatly appreciated. Throughout the next couple of months, we were blessed to have the opportunity to attend the NBA finals to see the Golden State Warriors play in game seven. They were Mike's all-time favorite team. When I met him, his childhood bedroom had Warriors wallpaper. We attended multiple San Francisco Giants games with front row seats, met players, and were given tours of AT&T Park. We were invited to spend the day with the San Francisco 49ers at their brand new stadium in Santa Clara, but at the time there was so much negativity with Colin Kaepernick and law enforcement, I politely declined that invitation.

When President Barack Obama came into Moffett Field, we met him and were given the opportunity to see Air Force One up close and personal. Even the secret service gave my boys their challenge coins, as well as the Air Force One pilot. Plus, the boys were given the same drink and food menu President Obama used on the plane that day. The boys also got to throw out the first pitch at a San Jose Giants baseball game and hang out with the players in the dugout, not to mention a complete Giants organization apparel store shopping spree.

The invites kept coming. So much so that we couldn't attend them all. I will forever be grateful to the individuals who made all those special outings possible. Yes, it absolutely sucks why we were given those opportunities. But seeing those smiles on the boys' faces as they screamed their heads off at the NBA playoffs and being tongue-tied when they met their favorite baseball players are positive memories they will never forget during a time of so many terrible ones.

There were also invites I wanted so desperately to ignore because I was in denial of what had become my new reality. One of those being therapy. A local organization called Dream-Power provides equine therapy on a ranch to law enforcement and military families. I had never been to any type of therapy before. I viewed it as something negative. Like there must be something wrong with you if you needed therapy. Mike and I attended a handful of premarital counseling sessions when we were engaged, but that was the extent of my experience.

All three of us went to counseling kicking and screaming. I have to say, though, it was one of the best resources we were given to help us work through our grief. Instead of being cooped up in an office with a stranger, we were all outside in the open air on a ranch with various types of animals and with professionals connected to our law enforcement family, helping us each work through our stages of grief. Over four years later, we occasionally attend DreamPower as we continue to work through our grief.

The rest of the summer passed, and it was time for school to start again. What I thought would be my plan for my own career and future was obviously a different plan than God had for me. My goal had been to be in administration at the school where I was currently teaching and the boys were attending. All those plans of mine quickly faded away. My priority was now the well-being of Josh and Jason. I made the difficult decision not to return to teaching in the fall.

For the first time in their young lives, the boys were going to attend school without their mom teaching on the same campus. Now with Jason entering the third grade and Josh fifth, they would be dropped off and picked up like the other kids at school. During their school days, I went nonstop with my meetings and obligations. Some days the boys didn't go to school and hung out with me wherever I needed to be, or I stayed home with them. I knew it was going to be a year of grace when it came to school, and I am so thankful our school allowed us all to have that.

Eventually, it came time for some of the hardest decisions for me to face. There was one task in particular that I needed to complete, and I continued to postpone it even though I knew it was inevitable. I had to write my victim impact statement to be read in court for the man who killed Mike.

As I prepared for that date, I made it clear to all lawyers and police personnel involved that I didn't want to know any details of the accident. In meetings, I would step out when those details were being discussed. I wouldn't read any police reports or paperwork that gave any details. To this very day, I still feel the same way.

When one hears an officer is killed in the line of duty, it is almost always associated with some form of murder or serious crime. Especially using the strong word *killed* makes one assume the most negative thoughts on how the officer could have lost his or her life. Often, it is plain, cold-blooded murder. With Mike, this was not the case.

Just a few weeks before Mike died, he came home from work raving about some churros he had eaten. He knew I loved churros and jokingly apologized to me that he ended up eating the one he got for me on his way home. He told me more about the nice "churro guy" who made these delicious churros. His partner knew him too. Mike and his partner stopped at the churro cart while on duty and had a conversation with the churro guy. He thanked them for their service and even sat on Mike's police bike and took pictures, as excited as a little boy would be.

Mike's death was not a murder; it was not intentional. It was an accident. The fact it was an accident was almost harder to cope with rather than it being a murder. Mike and his partner were almost at the end of their shift when they decided to make a quick stop before following each other back to Hollister which was where his partner lived also. Mike was at an intersection on his motorcycle getting ready to turn. He pulled out into the intersection when a van made an illegal left turn and hit Mike head on. I still do not know any more details besides just that. I do not know exactly how Mike died. I heard maybe he died in the ambulance on the way to the hospital. It was not until I got his death certificate that stated the cause of death was heart lacerations that I knew any other details. He looked so normal when I saw him that night at the hospital after the accident, so heart lacerations does make sense.

I am not sure when I will ever be ready to know the rest of the details of Mike's accident. I know our sons will want to know some day, and maybe that will be when I do it, for them. In the meantime, it hurts too much to think about my handsome and healthy husband being struck by another vehicle hard enough to be thrown off his bike and killed. There is one detail that I do know. I know the driver of the van. It was the churro guy.

I will never forget the day Mike's partner told me. He had come to check on us and to say hello to the boys. He and all Mike's motors buddies were really good about keeping in contact with us. We were standing around our cars in our driveway just talking. We got on the topic of Mike's accident, and that was when he told me the story of the churro guy. This was weeks after Mike had died. This whole time I had been oblivious not knowing it was this man who had killed my husband. I felt terrible.

I have only heard from people who were on the scene that as soon as this man realized it was Officer Katherman he had hit, the officer he had recently met, the same bike he had recently sat on, he lost it. He asked for someone to get his Bible out of his car because he needed to pray for Mike. This man was an elderly man who didn't speak English. Since there was that connection between him and Mike's partner, I continued to hear how distraught this man was. He truly was suffering because of what one wrong turn resulted in. It resulted in him taking my husband's life, someone he had recently met and respected.

With all the meetings, obligations, and decisions I was responsible for, I knew one of the biggest of them all was going to inevitably stare me in the face. It was the upcoming court date for the trial of the churro man. Leading up to the court date, I had multiple meetings with the lawyer representing Mike and the San Jose Police Department. With each meeting, we continued to discuss the possibilities of punishment for this man. We discussed if I was going to sue him. We discussed if I wanted to testify in court and make a statement. These were some of the meetings I absolutely dreaded. It was like a never-ending cycle of reliving that awful day.

The day of the court trial finally came. A day I was dreading. A day I knew I couldn't handle alone. My aunt Paulett drove up from Santa Maria, and one of my best friends from college, Lisa, flew out from the San Diego area to go with me for support. I had worked on writing my statement for weeks. My words were going to highly impact the judge's decision for the churro guy's punishment. I wrote and rewrote my statement over and over. I knew my words and my wishes would change this man's life forever. I had two options. I could have the book thrown at him for taking my husband's life, for taking my boys' father's life, for stealing our future, and for causing more pain than anyone will ever truly know. Or I could offer my forgiveness to this elderly man who was already suffering and must live with the fact that his actions killed a man, which could very well be punishment enough.

I was a nervous wreck that day. Paulett, Lisa, and I drove together to the courthouse near the police department where we met Derek and Anthony, along with a few of Mike's close police friends, command staff, and Mike's parents. We waited together outside the courtroom until it was time to enter. Besides having been involved in a program called Peer Court in high school, I had no experience with lawyers, judges, and courtrooms. We walked into the small courtroom and took our seats. I had never seen the driver of the van face to face; I had only read his name on court documents.

He sat in the front row next to his lawyer and his daughter who was translating for him. He kept his head down. I didn't realize when we took our seats, he was sitting directly in front of me. Once I realized this, my heart sank. I felt the mixed emotions of anger and compassion. Up to this point, he had already spent a short amount of time in jail and had been doing hours upon hours of community service voluntarily. My heart raced, and I felt nauseous as we followed the bailiff's order to rise as the judge entered the room. I kept thinking, *What the hell is happening? How am I sitting in a court room for the trial of the man who killed my husband, about to give a statement that may quite possibly shock everyone in the room?*

I was not quite sure when it would be my turn to approach the stand. The lawyers each took their turns. I couldn't keep my eyes off the man in front of me. I could tell by hearing his cries, seeing his tears and body language that he was a wreck. I'm sure he was nervous about his future and seeing the family of the officer he hit. His statement was translated and read, which made me cry. It was sincere and as apologetic as could be.

The stand to approach was in front of the judge and on the right side of where the defendant was sitting. I knew I was going to have to walk right past him to get there, and I would see him face to face when I returned to my seat. After many words from the judge, it was finally time for the widow of Officer Katherman to take the stand. Paulett and Lisa gave me the reassurance through their eyes and squeezing of my hand to tell me, "You've got this. You can do this."

I grasped my typed statement in my hand and proceeded down the middle aisle to the front of the courtroom. Yet another aisle of terror for me to walk down. All eyes were on the back of me as I spoke directly to the judge. While I was speaking, I kept having this distracting thought, hoping the whole time the back of my dress was properly situated and I was not giving a show to all who sat behind me. I am pretty sure I asked Paulett and Lisa after if my booty was showing as I was standing up there. It's weird how our brains work sometimes.

I hesitated to begin. I saw the court reporter pause in her typing to wait for me. I took a deep breath and slowly read my victim impact statement. I spoke about how my life and my future, and my boys' lives and their future had been completely turned upside down and taken from us. I choked back my tears as I read my typed notes stating that because of a wrong turn, my husband was never coming home. Many times, I had to pause to regroup, breathe, and bravely continue. I said I was angry and hated the fact that my sons will now have to grow up without their dad. I talked about how amazing Mike was, no *is*, and that his life was taken way too soon. It was not fair. I said I wanted to blame someone; I wanted to make sure someone had to pay for all the pain the boys and I will have to endure for the rest of our lives.

Then I said, but that is not what Mike would want. Besides my dad and grandpa, Mike was the most forgiving and generous man I had ever known. There was no foul play in his accident. There was no alcohol involved, no drugs, no texting while driving, no criminal record whatsoever of the driver, no speeding, no reckless driving. It was simply a wrong turn which put Mike's motorcycle and the van in the same place at the same time. How could I throw the book at an elderly eighty-something-year-old man who would most likely have to spend the rest of his life in jail for an accident?

I took a deep breath, looked right at the judge, and said, "Please give this man the absolute minimum sentence you can because he will have a life sentence of his own living with the memories and flashbacks of all that took place that afternoon on June 14. No jail time is going to bring my husband back. No amount of money he can be forced to pay me will bring my husband back. Please, your honor, just let him go."

As I was reading my statement I could hear the man's daughter whispering to him as she translated every word I said. I could hear his sobs. As I finished and turned around, I saw his face for the first time, soaked in tears. I knew I had made the right choice, and I knew Mike would have been proud of me. I walked back to my seat and felt a small sense of relief that another huge obstacle and stressor was finally done. I prayed that the judge would truly take the words from my heart into consideration as he made his final sentencing decision.

In the end, the driver of the van who killed my husband received the least punishment possible in a sentencing of killing a police officer. He was to serve no more jail time, complete a specified amount of community service hours, and pay a fee that would go to the courts and not to me. As his sentencing was read to him, I could see and hear the relief of both him and his daughter sitting in front of me. I could sense the awe of the people in the courtroom as they just witnessed a great act of forgiveness.

This act of forgiveness didn't come from me. It came from my Heavenly Father. What better way to be an example of Christ's love and honor my husband's godly and faithful life than to offer the same forgiveness that I am given each and every time I make a mistake or have an accident? When we forgive, we are forgiven too.

As court was adjourned, everyone who was in their seats slowly made their way out of the courtroom through the side double doors. Once I got to the doors, the churro guy, his daughter, and his lawyer all stood in front of me. First, his daughter came straight to me. She looked me in the eyes, said "thank you," and we cried together as we hugged. His lawyer was next, who told me she couldn't believe this outcome and hugged me as well. I then locked eyes with this man who was the reason why my whole world had been turned upside down. My heart was broken because of him. My boys will never play basketball, go fishing, or get a big bear hug from their dad ever again here on this earth because of him. This man was the reason my husband was dead.

This man and I held each other tight as we both sobbed in each other's arms. In his best, mostly broken English, he looked me in the eyes and said, "I am so sorry. I am so sorry for your sons."

I told him, "I know you are. Thank you." In that moment, I knew I had made the right choice. Was it easy to forgive this man? Absolutely not. Was it easy for Jesus to be beaten, tortured, and killed for my sins? Absolutely not. But He loves me so much more than He loved Himself to the point that He did the unthinkable to prove it to me. I love Mike so much that I did the unthinkable to bring honor to his legacy and glory to God's name. It was a day I will never forget. A day I know I was able to make Mike proud.

Chapter 12

Rebuilding the Life I Never Wanted

Leaving Derek and Morgan's house was difficult, but I knew the kids and I needed some time together to figure things out. All three of us trying to live in a hotel room was quite the challenge, I'll admit. I had a makeshift kitchen set up. Clothes that people had donated or purchased for us I organized as best I could in the six-drawer hotel dresser and tiny closet to share. More plastic bins and trash bags of clothes were piled in the corner. The tiny hotel desk was stacked with what looked like organized chaos of flood insurance paperwork, police department paperwork, and the boys' schoolwork. We ate the complimentary hotel breakfast every morning before I would take the boys to school. I had different friends who would send an extra lunch with their children to school for the boys or purchase them hot lunch. Friends would bring dinner to us or invite us over for dinner in the evenings, and I would also typically bring a load of laundry with me.

I didn't have any family who lived in the same town as the boys and I did. True friends show up in time of need, and boy, mine did. I was beyond grateful, yet filled with guilt as well. It had been six months, and I was finally starting to drive myself again, run my own errands, cook meals for us, trying my best to rebuild this new, unchartered life, then BAM! My legs were swept out from under me again, and I was struggling to stay afloat. This time the water was real.

My friends never even hesitated to help us again. The donations, gift cards, use of vehicles (since mine were destroyed in the flood), taking in our animals, fundraisers, meals, clothes, replacing electronics—you name it, we were well taken care of. At the end of each day, I would lay in that queen hotel bed with my boys on either side of me, silently crying and begging God to let them be okay. Most nights I would carefully and slowly peel myself out from under them and tiptoe to that tiny hotel bathroom, collapse on the cold floor, and sob with the fan on so they couldn't hear me. Sometimes on the floor in the bathroom, I would call Paulett, Lisa, Morgan, my sister or my mom, the women who held me together, to whom I vented my sorrows. I am not sure if anyone, not even those five, really knew how utterly broken I was.

I was already battling the "why" questions with God. Why did my boys have to lose their dad? Why did I have to lose my husband? Why our family, God? Again, I couldn't wrap my head around why God would allow another tragedy to happen to us. Why did my boys have to experience those terrifying moments of the flood? Why am I alone with them through all of this? Why our house? Why is Mike not here to help me? The questions were endless.

I had no choice but to get myself out of bed each day, get out of the tiny hotel room, try to make the days as normal as possible for the boys, and face the next trial ahead. The myriad of trials following the natural disaster that destroyed my home and the nightmare that destroyed my heart were unimaginable. I could never manage all that lay ahead on my own. Never.

It has been four months since I've journaled. If my life wasn't already a living hell, the most unexpected tragedy, a second one has happened again. Our home flooded. The details of this could be a whole journal in itself. I am so glad this little journal survived the flood. I had it in the drawer of my nightstand. I still don't know how I am functioning or getting through each day. I think this quote pretty much sums it up: "You don't know how strong you really are until you have no other choice but to be strong." This is so true. I have never seen myself as strong. I never had to be. I had an amazingly strong husband who was strong enough for the both of us. But now I have no choice. It's just me, and I have to be strong for our boys. I don't want to be. I want to curl up in my bed day after day and just cry, but I can't. Maybe I'll look back on this journal and can use all this pain and all these months of hell to minister to someone else someday.

Each day crews of people suited up in rubber boots, gloves, and some even face masks would meet at my house to clear loads and loads of muddy, unsalvageable memories from the soggy remains of our home. My close friends, their friends, local law enforcement from San Jose and other agencies, and strangers, tirelessly took load after load to the dump or wiped down and sanitized anything that could possibly be salvageable and go to a local storage unit. Friends took boxes of pictures and photo albums and hung them to dry on clotheslines in their garage. Mike's guns were taken to the police department's gun range to be cleaned. All our dirt bikes were hauled off to be quickly taken apart and cleaned and saved from all the water damage.

Within days the house and barn were completely cleared out, mud scraped, and power washed. Drywall was cut from the floor to the top of the highest water lines and sanitized; insurance claims were filed; contractors' bids were given to re-build. I was ready to face the challenge of getting us back into our home even if it took months and months to rebuild. But God had other plans.

As each new storm came through, the waters rose in the broken levee and flooded my home and property again. My home flooded five times. Some of the sequential flood waters rose higher than the first. Getting to the property was only possible in a four-wheel-drive raised vehicle but not guaranteed. I got stuck and had to be pulled out more than once. It was a good thing I had experience four-wheeling with Mike. Each day I four-wheeled through mud pits to get to my house. I switched my shoes for rubber boots before getting out of the truck, put my gloves on, and held my breath. The stench was terrible of the nasty dried mud and soggy ponds now surrounding my home.

I never took the boys with me any of these times. I couldn't imagine having them see their home in the condition it was in. Eventually, it was officially red tagged by the county and deemed uninhabitable. There would be no rebuilding our dream farmhouse. There would be no decked-out barn the way Mike had planned. There would be no more shooting gophers with the pellet gun off the back porch or riding dirt bikes after school before starting homework. There would be no more watching sunsets from the tractor seat bench Mike made for us. There would be no more memories to be made there.

When the county forbid me to enter my home, I realized I couldn't rebuild our lives there. I felt so defeated, like I had let Mike down, and all the volunteers who remodeled our home, all for it to be destroyed. I already walked away from my husband's body lying in a casket to be buried in the ground without me there because I couldn't bear to see it. Now I had to walk away and leave the home we were supposed to raise our boys in and make our forever home, and I couldn't bear to do that either.

For months it sat there, as did all the homes and land on Lovers Lane. It was a sight of deserted wreckage up and down the once-beautiful country road. While I waited for insurance claims to process, the boys and I moved from the tiny hotel room to a small one-bedroom apartment in town. Our amazing friends set us up with beds. We borrowed couches. We were in a top-floor apartment because my boys were afraid of flooding again. Jason only slept on the top bunk because he was afraid of waking up to water. Fear consumed me. All I wanted was to protect my boys from more heartache, and I felt like I was failing miserably.

With no plans on what to do with our once-beautiful, now

uninhabitable home or where to go once the six-month lease was up in the apartment, I gave my worries to the Lord. He allowed for all this to happen, and I knew He was not going to leave us stranded.

John and Jennifer, our realtors, helped me list the Lovers Lane property. We didn't know who in their right mind would buy a shell of a house in the middle of a flood zone surrounded by standing water now filled with snakes, floating port-a-potties, trash, and contamination with feces from farm animals and sewage from the homes. But God knew.

People came and looked at the property, but no one was ready for this challenge. There was going to be so much red tape to get through the county to make the home habitable again. An investor came and looked at the property. He flipped homes for a living and was determined to flip our dilapidated home. I was skeptical with how serious he was on making an offer on this as-is sale. With the money from my insurance claim and the investor's offer, it was possible to break even on the sale of the home. No short sale, no foreclosure. A clean break from a possible financial disaster. Of course, God did not stop at just breaking even.

I accepted the offer and was able to pay off what we owed on the house and even had a little left over. Enough to start a new tradition.

I used that small amount of leftover money for the boys and me to take a trip to Maui to celebrate Mike's birthday that October. Maui was one of Mike's favorite places. He had gone multiple times growing up with his parents and brother, and we went there on our honeymoon and my thirtieth birthday. Finally, something positive for the three of us. A little getaway from all the uncertainty that was our lives to a place filled with happy memories. We have continued the tradition and have gone back every October for Mike's birthday week.

Eventually, it was getting closer to the end of the lease on our small apartment. A good friend of mine, Natalie, was always willing and ready to help us with anything we needed. Finding a home for us to not only settle down in but to feel safe in was her goal. With her connections to our community, she was able to pair us with the most generous family in town who offered us one of their newly flipped homes to rent.

It was a quaint, newly remodeled three-bedroom, two-bath house in a safe neighborhood and walking distance from the boys' school. It was also right next door to a retired San Jose police lieutenant whose family soon became like family to us. Once we moved in, I started to decorate to make it feel as homey as I could for the boys. We finally felt safe. We were able to bring our dog Roxy back home, which was so important to the boys.

Even though we were in a real home again, and the boys were starting to get a sense of normalcy, nothing felt normal to me. This was the first home without Mike. There were no memories under this roof with him. My new reality slapped me in the face again. While grateful for this beautiful new roof over our heads, I was still lost, defeated, and broken. I was rebuilding a life I never wanted.

By this time, we were getting closer to rounding out our first full year after losing Mike. I was still dealing with different responsibilities associated with the police department, and we were coming up on our first experience with being the family of a fallen officer in the month of May. During the month of May, ceremonies honoring our local, state, and nation's fallen officers are held all over the country. With it being Mike's first year after his End of Watch, we traveled to ceremonies around the Bay Area, California's ceremony in Sacramento, and Washington, DC, for national ceremonies.

On the plane ride to DC, I took out my journal and wrote exactly how I was feeling on the five-hour flight to honor my husband in our nation's capital.

> *May 11, 2017*
>
> *I am on the plane to Washington, DC, for National Police Week. Seriously!? We are going to be there attending multiple ceremonies to honor Mike. Last week we were in Sacramento for the California memorial . . . again, seriously? I think I was numb the whole time in Sacramento, or maybe my antidepressants I am now on make me have no emotion. Maybe I have just gone through way too many memorials and somber ceremonies this year that I am just over all of this. You would think with almost eleven months having passed that I would have filled up numerous journals. For some reason it's just so hard for me to sit down and write. So hard to relive everything, but I feel like I need to for the boys. They're going to have so many questions someday. I fear that I won't have the answers. I feel like I fail as a mom daily. Mike would have done such a better job raising the boys. I am not sure how I'm going to do this by myself. I'm molding these boys into young men, but there's no man in our house. Why, God, why?*

After more than two weeks of somber ceremonies hearing "Officer Michael J. Katherman, End of Watch, June 14, 2016," over and over, his name added to the list of fallen officers of 2016, I felt a huge sense of relief during the flight back home from DC. I was looking forward to getting back to our new house, which was starting to feel a little more like home, and enjoy the beginning of summer with the boys. We even had a trip planned to Disneyland with my sister-in-law and niece, Legoland, and to my bestie Lisa's house near San Diego for the week of Mike's first End of Watch and Father's Day. We had something to look forward to.

But, when we returned from the fun getaway, we were met with another punch in the gut. We walked inside the house and put our suitcases down. The three of us were doing our own things around the house when I made my way to use the hallway bathroom. I walked in and couldn't believe my eyes. The entire ceiling over the shower had collapsed into the bathtub, leaving a huge gaping hole in the ceiling and a gigantic mess. It was late on a Sunday evening, and I had no clue who to call or what to do. Apparently, there had been a leak in the pipes. Flood flashbacks came, and I saw the fear in my boys' eyes once again worrying about what were we going to do. *Come on, God—can't a girl catch a break?* is all I could think. Just as we were starting to get into our groove and doing a little better in our healing process, we were pulled down again.

Eventually, the construction began, and the homeowners had the whole house re-piped, which meant we were living in a construction zone again. This time, though, I was thankful to be a renter, having all the details taken care of for me.

All three of us were still attending therapy at DreamPower each week. There were so many times either Josh or Jason didn't want to attend, nor did I, but I knew I had to make them, and I had to force myself to go as well. The two of them were struggling big time and in complete opposite ways. Josh, my oldest, was emotional and sad. He never wanted me out of his sight. He would get upset if I walked into the garage without telling him. That is how attached he was to me. I am sure he was afraid something may happen to his mom, too, and she would never come back like his dad.

Jason was full of rage and anger. His lash-outs were terrifying. He would scream at me, telling me he hated me, and he threatened to kill himself more than once. As the months went by, things would get better for a week or so for both boys, and then they would each fall back into their own traps of grief. It was utterly exhausting for me. Even though I still had my amazing support system of local friends, I still felt so alone. A very broken mom trying to parent two very broken boys was far too much to handle. They needed their dad, and nothing I could do was filling that void for them. I exhausted every grief resource I knew trying to help them.

Holding my son at night while he sobbed for his daddy; trying to control my boy as he raged in anger because his dad died and he wants to know why; having my son get into the car after school and lose it because all the other kids got picked up by their dads and his doesn't anymore; it all crushed me. Not being able to change the channel in time before the boys saw another news clip about their dad's crash pissed me off. Having my sons afraid at night because it was only the three of us in the house made me frightened too. Hearing people's judgment on decisions I made for our family when they'd never been in my shoes hurt.

I was so wrapped up in making sure the boys were okay and healing in a positive way that I never stopped to focus on myself. Over a year of nonstop anguish took its toll. Now a year and a half after losing my husband, I couldn't do this life on my own any longer. I couldn't raise these boys by myself. They needed more. They needed a happy and healthy mom, and they desperately needed their dad.

It took a long time and a lot of persuasion from my best friends and family, but I finally agreed to make myself a priority along with my boys. They convinced me that if I didn't, I wouldn't be able to help them like I so desperately desired. I began to open up more in therapy. I started journaling more. I tried hard to eat regularly again. I even went out to dinner with my girlfriends a few times.

Most importantly, I slowly started to resume attending church. For quite some time, I couldn't get through a worship song without sobbing. Still, in the midst of it all, something was missing. These boys needed more, but I didn't know what more would be.

As much as I could, I spent time at the cemetery with Mike. I would sit on my blanket talking to him, praying to God, laughing to myself, and sobbing. There was a particular day I was a mess. I lay on that blanket sobbing, face down. Not caring who saw me. I was done. Done trying to be so strong for everyone else. I sobbed while telling Mike I couldn't do this. I was letting him down. I begged him, out loud, to send me someone, even though I had no idea what or who I needed.

Please God, send me someone to love my boys like Mike did. Send me someone to take care of us. Send me someone he would approve of to live this new life with. I laid on the blanket for what felt like hours, praying to God and asking Mike for his help. I remember specifically telling God it could be tomorrow or years from now; just please, in Mike's time and in God's time, make the three of us happy again.

Soon after, I met David.

Chapter 13

Check Yes or No

Over a year passed since we lost Mike. I didn't know what I wanted or what I needed. Something I did know was that I didn't want to end up alone. I feared I was going to be too much for someone. That my heartbroken boys were going to be too much. That my story was going to be too much. Who would be interested in someone with all my baggage? I was thirty-three when I became a widow, but I couldn't imagine loving anyone else but Mike.

When I filled out certain paperwork requiring me to choose my marital status, I was confused on what I was supposed to check. I didn't know if I should put married or single. To me, I was still married. Mike and I didn't get a divorce. We didn't choose to not be married anymore. Why was I instantly considered a single woman on paper? I hated choosing that option. Occasionally, *widowed* would be an option, and that was just a slap in the face. A single, widowed thirty-four-year-old was not what I wanted on paper, let alone in real life.

I was conflicted about my wedding ring. I was still wearing it every day on my ring finger. I had no intention of taking it off. I remember attending a meeting with multiple other widows, and I quickly noticed I was the only one still wearing my wedding ring. Some had turned theirs into other pieces of jewelry or wore them on a chain around their necks. Others had tucked them away for their children. I will never forget scanning the hands in the room and realizing I was the only one wearing her ring. I am now embarrassed to say that I judged them all. *How could they move on so quickly? Don't they still love their husbands who died?* I was so naïve.

I remember telling my friends Heather and Natalie about it. Then my time came. It was a topic in therapy I wrestled with each week. I would wear it on my ring finger for a couple of days, switch hands, wear it around my neck on a chain with Mike's wedding band, or not wear it at all. Sometimes it would depend on where I was going. If I was with family, I would wear it on my wedding ring finger. When I was with my close group of friends, I would try to wear it on a chain around my neck. I was conflicted and no choice I made each day ever felt right. I loved my wedding set. It was beautiful.

The guilt I felt when I was not wearing it overwhelmed me. I also wondered what people would think. I worried way too much about what others thought about the decisions I made. Would they be as naïve as I was and think if I were not wearing my ring, it must mean I have moved on and don't love Mike anymore? Absolutely ludicrous.

On our wedding day, we stood before God, our family, and our friends, and vowed "until death do us part." To a twenty-one-year-old couple, those words meant until we were old, gray, and on our deathbeds together. It didn't mean until we were in our early thirties. What it meant for me was guilt, confliction, and confusion. How is it instantly normal to be a single, wedding-ring-free woman after sixteen years being Mike's best friend, girlfriend, fiancée, and wife? Everything I knew and defined myself as was stripped away from me.

One evening I was talking to one of my best friends, Jamie, on the phone. Jamie lived in Alabama at the time and had known me for over twenty years. She knew I needed a nudge to venture into the dating world again. I kept telling her there was no way. Where in the world would I meet anyone? I was a single mom with two boys. My life revolved around them—their school, their sports, their social lives, and their mental sanity. That's all I had time for. Jamie told me I should try a dating website. Again, "No way," I told her. I laughed at the thought of it. And what would someone think if they even saw me on it? I was always thinking about what others thought. I wish I would have realized sooner that all that really matters is what God thinks and if what I am doing would be okay with Mike and make him proud of me. I was the only one who could answer that.

Finally, her encouraging approval talked me into it. I told her I would sign up for Match.com for twenty-four hours. That's it. I would see what happened, and then I'd be done. That Friday night, I set up a vague profile. I never used my name. I posted only one picture of myself in a baseball hat and wearing sunglasses. I wanted it to be as incognito as could be. Besides Jamie, I told no one. There was no way I was going to allow anyone to judge me. I was only doing this to prove a point to Jamie that it was a dumb idea.

Once my simple, with hardly-any-details-about-myself profile was live, I received message after message from stranger after stranger. It was weird. I felt like I was doing something wrong. It was also kind of fun. Fun to laugh at some of the messages that popped in. At the dorky pickup lines some guys would send. At how ridiculous this was. How would I ever consider talking to, let alone meet in person, some strange man I met online? I answered a few of the questions I received then called it a night.

The next morning, I sat out in our backyard in my teal high-backed chair with my cup of coffee and my computer on my lap while the boys played on the trampoline. This was the week after I had cried out to Mike and the Lord to help the boys and me to be happy again. I was browsing online and checking my email. I had multiple messages in my inbox all filtered through Match.com. I opened them one by one, rolling my eyes, and also giggling at the comments. With each click of a new message, I presumed it would be another creepy guy trying his catfish hand at a lame pickup line. I continued browsing while the boys played, and I opened another email that caught me off guard as I read words full of kindness and sincerity.

This message was unlike any other I received. This person politely introduced himself. He told me I had a pretty smile and said he would understand if I chose not to respond. He continued to say he had never put himself out there like this and was nervous to contact me. This online platform was new to him, and he didn't even have a picture posted. There was something in those words that made me feel like they were genuinely written. There was no cheesy pickup line, no instant asking to meet up with me; it just felt different from the others.

I read the message feeling confused, yet curious. I was not sure if I should respond. His not knowing anything about me made me feel a sense of relief. He had no clue who I was. He didn't know whose widow I was or the story behind it all. That was so refreshing. I worked up the nerve to send back a short response. Later that morning, he replied to my message, and we messaged back and forth a couple of more times. My twenty-four-hour bet with Jamie was almost up. I ended up giving this mystery man with no picture my email address.

The emails back and forth became more and more frequent, almost like a text conversation. As we began to share little tidbits of our hobbies and childhoods—still no details of who I was or even names—I became more intrigued. It felt nice to talk to someone, to have interest shown in me and to be pursued a little even if it was through email. The most important detail of all was he was a Christian. He knew Jesus, loved Jesus, and it showed in even our earliest written conversations. This is the reason why he was so different from the rest.

Over the next few days, we exchanged numbers and began to text. He still didn't know my last name or my story, though I found out his name was David. The texting continued on throughout each day and late into each night. He finally did send me a picture of himself, and even though I liked who I was talking to so far, I was relieved to see how handsome he was. The texting gave me a little bit of excitement each day. Something to look forward to. A little secret I was keeping that was bringing a smile to my face and happy thoughts, which were much needed and a welcome change.

Still just two people getting to know more about each other, we eventually started having phone conversations. By now I knew he was divorced and had two kids, who at the time were five and seven. One girl and one boy. By now he knew I was a widow and had two kids as well. We would each put our kids to bed for the night and talk for hours, getting to know more and more about each other. Our phone conversations would begin around 9:00 p.m. and sometimes last until 3:00 a.m., with him having to get ready for work shortly after. I guess the adrenaline and excitement of our conversations kept us awake through our days after staying up all night on the phone. Still never meeting face to face, him still not knowing my story, I started to wonder what in the world I was doing talking this much to a stranger I met on a twenty-four-hour stint with Match.com. The feelings of both butterflies and guilt confused me. I was interested in this man I was getting to know, but I felt so guilty at the same time. I felt like I was cheating on Mike. I felt like I was doing something wrong. I kept everything to myself and didn't even tell my closest friends or family right away. Most nights I would go into my walk-in closet, sit on the floor and talk to him on the phone because I didn't want my boys to hear me and question why I was on the phone all night or ask who I was talking to.

One night while we were talking, I decided to be completely honest and tell him my whole story. I shared with him the details that led me to becoming a widow. I told him about the devastating flood. I told him I was still healing. I told him my boys' world had been turned completely upside down, and I didn't want them to know I was talking to someone; I didn't plan on introducing them to another man anytime soon. He listened, he understood, and he told me my story was not going to scare him away.

He told me he would love to continue getting to know me. He remembered hearing our whole story on the news. He finally knew who I really was. It was a relief, yet still a worry. A relief to get it all out and a worry that he would soon realize what being with me would really entail and want nothing to do with me. I thought I was damaged goods.

We knew we wanted to meet in person, but we weren't sure how to make that happen. We lived an hour away from each other, and I had two kids I was not ready to share this new part of my life with just yet. I was scared and nervous, yet excited. There were so many ups and downs and ranges of emotions for both of us. We were both coming from broken marriages—one broken by divorce and one broken by death. We both had children to put first in any decisions we made.

We finally were able to coordinate our schedules and make sure our kids were taken care of. Both of us not knowing what to expect, both of us not knowing what it would be like to go on a first date again, and both of us nervous to finally meet each other face to face for the first time, we set our first date. Now I just had to wait. I felt excitement mixed with fear. We were like two giddy teenagers. We knew more about each other than anyone could imagine or even comprehend, and we still had not even met.

I finally told my sister and a couple of my closest friends about our upcoming first date. *Who is this guy? Are you sure you are ready for this? What if he is not who he says he is? Check in throughout the day so we know you are safe.* Their reactions were of both excitement for me and hesitation, yet they trusted my judgment and encouraged me when I questioned myself.

As our date grew closer, I was getting more nervous. I worried about the most trivial things. *What was I going to wear? What if someone I knew saw me out on a date? What if he saw me and was disappointed? What if he didn't like me after hanging out in person? What if I didn't like him? What do I talk about?* It had been seventeen years since I had been on a first date, and I didn't know how this all worked anymore. And then the ultimate question: *What would Mike think?*

All of the decisions I was making during this new experience didn't come without fervent prayer and seeking guidance from the Lord. I was scared. This was not just my life that I was putting out there. This could very well affect my boys' lives as well. I was afraid for them. With every decision I made, they came first.

The big day came. Of course, I didn't sleep much the night before, partly because of nerves, and partly because he and I talked on the phone most of the night. We made plans to meet a few blocks away from my house in a school parking lot. I didn't want the boys or our friend who was watching them to see me getting picked up by a guy. He also still didn't know where I lived, and I wanted to keep it like that for now. As I finished getting ready, I got a text from him, letting me know he was at the school.

Butterflies, nerves, and worry took over. I made my way to meet him, and as I drove around the corner, I saw the truck he described in the parking lot. There he was. This was really happening. No turning back now. I pulled into that parking lot, and I was so excited to get out of my car to finally see this guy I had been falling for. I had played this moment over and over in my mind. *Do I shake his hand? Do I give him a high five? Do I hug him? No way I can kiss him. What if I want to kiss him? Is it okay to kiss him?* My biggest questions of all: *What in the world was I doing? Am I making a big mistake?*

He got out of his truck, and I got out of my car, and none of those questions mattered the second I laid eyes on him. He wrapped his big, strong arms around me and hugged me for what felt like hours. I was instantly calm and knew I didn't want to be anywhere else but right there with him.

He opened his tailgate and had the sweetest surprises waiting for me. I love surprises. Beautiful flowers, not one package of double-stuffed Oreo cookies, but two, a couple of books for us to read together, and the sweetest card I had ever read.

Hey Beautiful,

The day has come, and I can't remember when I ever felt this excited, nervous, and anxious to meet someone. God is good, and all I can do is thank Him for crossing our paths. I pray every morning that this will work between us, and you don't run away today after we meet. So I guess if this card is open, then I made the cut! I got you a little something. Some cookies to go along with the books I hope we can read together to ground the start of our relationship. The flowers, well I fully know they will die in the truck today, but all I want to see is that smile on your face. I hope I can put that same smile on your face every day. I don't think I need this day ahead of us to know that I am in 100%, and I guess all that is left is to ask you to make this official. Will you be my girl? Check yes or no. P.S. See what I did there? Using a George Straight song to make us official.

Without a moment of hesitation, I checked yes as fast as

his pen would let me write. I knew in that moment this was it. Because on that day . . . I went on my last first date. The day my last chapter began.

Chapter 14

Our Last Chapters

After our first face-to-face meeting, our nerves settled, and we were finally off onto our first official date. My boys and his son and daughter were taken care of until the evening, so we headed off down the coast to Carmel with the whole day ahead of us. I left my car in the school parking lot where we met, and he drove us in his truck. Not too long on our drive, I got a text from Josh asking me why my car was parked in the school parking lot. He thought I was with friends. Busted. He was with a friend, and they drove past the school. I told him I met my friend there, and "she" drove us. Only a little white lie, right?

During the long drive to our first stop, there was no lack of conversation and laughs. Thank goodness because I was so afraid I was going to be awkward and have no clue what to say or even how to act. I didn't have much experience in the dating world. Before I met Mike at eighteen, my dad didn't allow me to go on dates alone with boys, so even then at thirty-five, I was like an awkward young girl giggling at every comment, funny or not, and twirling her hair attempting to flirt.

I knew he had planned a day and evening in Carmel, but I didn't know where we were going exactly. Since I love surprises, it was both exciting and scary. I felt a sense of relief we were going some distance from the town I lived in. I was not ready for anyone to see me alone with a guy. Carmel is a popular destination, and my eyes were peeled for familiar faces the whole time. I remember thinking maybe I should have put a tracker on my phone, just in case this guy ended up being crazy! Less than a handful of friends knew I was on my first date, yet nobody knew where I was. Looking back, I still cannot believe how trusting I was of this man.

Our first stop was beautiful Mission Ranch. It is a hotel, restaurant, and wedding venue owned by Clint Eastwood. The grounds are gorgeous, yet I had only seen it in pictures or on TV. A place David didn't even know I had always wanted to visit. We had a delicious brunch and walked around the gorgeous property. While walking the property, we saw the staff setting up outside for a wedding. We both talked about how this would be a beautiful location to have a wedding, and in my head, I was thinking . . . maybe even our wedding someday. Sounds crazy to have those thoughts on a first date, but I knew. If any of my girlfriends were to tell me they wanted to marry the guy they went on one date with, I would think they were nuts.

Next stop was wine tasting through Carmel Valley. Again, never a lull in conversation. It was amazing how comfortable I felt with him, like we had always been together. He made me smile. I mean a genuinely happy smile that had not been seen on my face for an awfully long time. I didn't want the day to end. We parked ourselves at the last winery and sat, talked, and sipped our wine until it was time for our dinner reservation. Of course, another beautiful location, Rocky Point, on a cliff overlooking the ocean. We sat outside to eat, enjoyed the gorgeous sunset, delicious food, and continued getting to know each other better. He definitely pulled out all the stops for this first date, and I loved every second of it. It felt good to be pampered again, to be taken care of, to feel safe and loved.

At times I had to push negative thoughts out of my mind that would begin to creep in. The thoughts made me feel like I was doing something wrong even when I knew I was not. There was so much guilt weighing on me, and it was hard to push off. Guilt for leaving my boys with a babysitter so I could go on a date. Guilt for lying to them about who I was with and where I was going. Guilt because no one knew where I was or the details of what I was doing, let alone who I was with. Guilt for not thinking about Mike that day and for genuinely being happy. Guilt for having feelings for another man.

Eventually, it was time to head back home to my boys. We took advantage of every second together with more conversation, laughs, and getting to know even more about each other as we drove back to that little parking lot where my car was parked. We planned when we could see each other again. My heart was bursting. The butterflies never left my tummy, and I was smiling from ear to ear. There was just something about this man I knew was different. I knew I loved him on that very first date, which again is just nuts. I knew he was the one. I knew everyone in my life would think I was crazy. I knew God and Mike had sent him to me.

It was not long after I got home when my phone rang. He was home too, and we talked late into the night as we always did. What was next? We had so many hurdles to jump if this was going to work out. Only God could get us over each one. We talked about how we could make this work. When do we tell our kids? How do we fit dating into our schedules? Each obstacle had to be worked through carefully since this relationship was not just about us, but our children as well. Each obstacle came with a challenge, but we knew it would be worth it.

Almost once a week, David and I were able to squeeze in some kind of date. It was tricky to get all four of our kids taken care of while we snuck away, but amazingly, it worked out well every time. For our second date, David scored some major points. This baseball-loving, faithful Oakland A's fan didn't just get us tickets to see my favorite team, the San Francisco Giants, play, but he got us on the field, Row 1, touch-the-players kind of seats. And he met up with me looking so handsome, decked out in Giants gear.

We had the kind of seats where we would be seen on TV numerous times. Again, I told the boys a little white lie that I was going to the game with friends. As I sat there getting texts from Josh saying he was looking for me on TV, I had the reasons I was not sitting by any of my girlfriends ready for explaining if needed. *Lord, please do not show us on the Kiss Cam.* It was bad enough the elderly man who worked there and escorted us to our seats asked David if he was going to propose to me tonight. I was still living with this huge secret of dating someone, so by no means was anyone going to get glimpses of me in the stands on TV smiling, getting cozy with the cute guy sitting next to me, seeing us kiss on the Kiss Cam, or getting engaged on the jumbotron.

Finally, I filled in one of my best friends, Heather, on all the David details. She had the idea to go on a double date together to see a concert. I know she felt the need to meet this guy and scope him out a bit. So, she and her hubby, Rob, and David and I all went to this little place that hosts small concerts, and we saw an upcoming country artist named Dylan Scott perform. It was such a fun night. It was also David's first introduction to any of my friends. This relationship was getting serious fast, and we loved spending as much time together as we could.

Eventually, it was time to plan a date myself, so I scored some awesome Florida Georgia Line tickets, which was David's favorite country group. Again, we had Heather and Rob join us, and we even met up with one of his sisters, Jessica, who I was able to meet for the first time that night. Another date on the books and another amazing time spent together.

I knew my parents needed to be one of the first family members I told about what I had been doing the last couple of weeks. They had no clue I was talking to David, let alone dating anyone. I called them on the phone one night after I put the boys to bed. I asked my mom to put my dad on the phone too. While on speaker, I told them both I had started talking to someone, and we had gone on a couple of dates. Before I could explain any further, my mom stopped me. In her shaky voice, trying her best to hold back her tears, she told me she needed to go and pretty much hung up on me. I was crushed. Of all the people, how could my mom and dad be upset with me? I was worried, and I was sad. It made me instantly question everything. They had lost a son when Mike died. I knew they were still grieving too.

A couple of hours later, my mom called me back. I was beyond relieved because I had had it all wrong. The reason why she was on the verge of tears and needed to hang up was not because she was mad or disappointed in me. She was so happy and relieved that she needed to hang up so she could go cry . . . happy tears. She told me it was all she and my dad had been praying for. They had been praying I would eventually meet someone sooner rather than later who would make me and the boys happy again. When she heard all about David and the excitement in my voice, they couldn't believe their prayers had been answered.

I was nervous to tell more family and close friends. I worried so much about what they would think. For some reason I thought everyone was going to be mad or disappointed in me. Most of all, I didn't want anyone to think I was over Mike, that I didn't still love him, or I was moving on too soon. The list went on and on of all the lies I was building up in my head. Yet, with each person I told, I received more support, more love, and more genuine excitement for me. I know both of us were still hesitant to make our new relationship public, especially since the most important people in both our lives still didn't know: our children.

There were four precious kids who had to come first. Each set of kids had their worlds turned upside down already—my boys losing their dad, and David's son and daughter losing the marriage of their parents. Each of our new families of three were finally getting settled and into a new groove of life, and we were afraid to upturn all of it again. We weren't sure how they would react to the approaching changes.

I had a feeling my boys would be the ones to hate this new relationship, especially Josh, who was still trying to be the man of the house and take care of me. He was very protective and incredibly attached to me. Each time I left for a few hours to go out with David, it was hard for him. Not because of who

I was with—he still didn't know anything about David—but because anytime I would leave him was really hard. I knew it was also good for him to have little breaks from me. And boy did I need them myself.

After fervent prayer, long talks together, therapy sessions on this topic, advice from my parents and our closest friends who knew our situation, we decided it was time to start the process of introducing my boys to David, David's kids to me, and our kids to one another. This decision was made only after careful consideration. This was quite the process, but it went more smoothly than we could have ever expected or hoped for, given our respective situations.

We followed the steps and timeline we were advised to use, and it was incredibly successful. We began with me not hiding in the closet after the boys went to bed to talk to David on the phone. I started talking to him on the phone or texting him out in the open in front of the boys. When they asked who I was talking to, because they always did, I replied with a simple, "Oh, it's just my friend David."

It started to become a daily routine, and I would soon be asked, "Mom, are you talking to your friend David?"

Next, I would talk about David to them.

"Hey, boys, remember my new friend David? Did you know he used to be a baseball pitcher like both of you?"

"That's cool, mom."

"He has a son named Brayden who likes sports and video games like you guys. We should plan a playdate sometime."

Here is an important part: I continued to talk like this about a couple of different friends we knew; therefore, it didn't seem like my conversations or comments were always focused on this new stranger mom had started talking to.

The first time the boys met David, it was only him. We didn't involve his kids just yet. I hosted a small barbeque at my house and invited some friends, including him. It was very casual, and to the boys he seemed to blend in like all the other guests, yet they were finally able to put a face to the name and become more comfortable with one of mom's new friends. Later, I asked the boys if they would like to have David and his kids over to play. They were excited to have a playdate with new friends, so that is what we did, and that is what we called it.

David, his son, Brayden, and daughter, Tegan, all came over. They played in the backyard, jumped on the trampoline, played video games, and rode on skateboards, everything kids would do together on a playdate. They all had a great time, and soon they asked when they could play again. We continued to plan different times to get the kids together to play or go somewhere fun. One time we met at Bass Pro Shop to go bowling; another time we met for ice cream or went swimming at David's pool. It all was very casual, and everyone seemed to get along. It was just like getting to know any new family we make friends with.

Each week in therapy, I updated my therapist on the progress, and we brainstormed another safe way to continue to ease David and his children into the boys' lives. I already knew this was something special. I already knew I was in love with this man. I already knew he was going to be my last chapter. Convincing Josh and Jason of the same was my biggest fear. As much as everything was going as planned, there were some setbacks, and as I suspected, they came from my boys.

Josh had major separation anxiety. Therefore, hanging out all of us together was perfectly fine and something he really enjoyed. As soon as I made plans to meet up with David without him, or even go out with my girlfriends, it was a big deal.

I mean like a panic attack, anxiety, scared-my-mom-is going-to-die-like-my-dad big deal. This was something we all had to continue to talk through in therapy, and I had to be very careful with leaving him for short periods at a time with someone he was comfortable with. I had to slowly work my way up to being able to be away from him for longer times to go on a decent date with David. Each time I would leave him, my phone wouldn't stop with texting and calls from him asking me my every detail of what I was doing or when I was coming home. It was a fine line I was dealing with. I needed to be sensitive to all that my son was going through but without enabling the behavior. Instead, I needed to guide him through getting better.

Eventually, the boys started to notice on their own that David and I liked each other. I am sure the smile that had returned to their mom's face and her less depressed attitude was easy to spot as well. They had already begun to develop a friendship with him, as well as Brayden and Tegan, which helped them both accept the idea of us becoming boyfriend and girlfriend.

David soon became a steady figure in the boys' life and the one who brought the smile to my face. It felt good to be happy again. It felt good to be loved again. To feel safe again. As the months went by, I began to tell more people in my life about this new relationship. Each time I did so with hesitation of the response I would receive. Each time the response was pure joy and happiness for me. The support I received from my closest family and friends was the relief I needed and confirmation I was making the right choices for me and the boys.

It didn't take long before David and I knew we wanted to blend our families together into one and get married. There were so many things that needed to happen before we could make that happen. He lived an hour away, and I was pretty set on not moving. My boys needed all the stability they could get, and after losing their dad and their home in the same year, I was not going to have them lose their school and friends as well. Thank the Lord, David completely understood that. He was set to move out of his house at the end of the year anyway, and his children's school only went up to second grade. Brayden would be entering third grade soon, and they would need to find a new school anyway. So, the option that made the most sense was for David and his kids to move to Gilroy, where the boys and I lived.

The depth of our relationship with each other, the bond our children already had together, the trust his children had for me and mine for him, and the support of our family made it seem like we had been in this relationship putting forth the effort to make it all work for years. It had only been months. From the day we met face to face, to the day David proposed was four months. I knew after the first moment I jumped into his arms and saw him face to face. I was finally going to feel love and happiness again.

His proposal was perfect. A fairytale, movie-perfect scene was set in the backyard of the new house we had just purchased. The house he and his kids moved into while the boys and I stayed in our rental. After one of our date nights, we went back to the house. As we walked in the door, he handed me a scarf and told me to use it as a blindfold. He led me to the backyard. All I could hear was music playing, and I could see faint lights through the scarf. My back was turned to the yard. He was already such a romantic, so I was not sure if this was a proposal or if he was just being the sweet guy who spoiled me. Later I did find out he had enlisted the help of his sister, Cheryl, and one of my besties, Heather. Regardless, they all made the backyard a magical setting I never wanted to leave.

He removed the scarf from my eyes, took my hands, and we danced to our song. As the song finished, he turned me around. The backyard was draped in twinkle lights, and lanterns lined the perimeter of the grass. Pictures of us and our newly blended family were strung with lights, and there were roses and wine. A wooden sign was made with our initials, and sitting under it, on a log, was an open ring box with glimmers of light beaming off the diamond held inside. David got down on his knee, took my hand, and asked me to be his wife, his last chapter.

With happy tears in my eyes, I said, "Yes!" I was so, so happy. He slipped the gorgeous ring on my finger; it was stunning. When he stood up, I jumped into his arms and kissed him under the beautiful twinkle lights in the backyard of this new house we would soon make a home for our new family. Even though I said yes, I knew this time there was so much more I was saying yes to. I was saying yes to becoming a wife, yet still I was a widow. This would be one of my life's biggest challenges and biggest blessings. I said yes to gaining two more children and becoming a bonus mom. I said yes to my boys having another dad—a dad on earth. I said yes to loving another man other than Mike. I said yes to faith—a deep faith that God was in control and leading us every step of the way as we navigated this new life together.

Yes.

Chapter 15

○

Two Families Become One

It was time to tell our kids the exciting news. Once I got back home to my boys after our amazing evening, they were already asleep. My plan was to tell them when they woke up in the morning, and I couldn't wait. I knew my oldest was somewhat aware because David told me he had talked to him about it. A couple of days before, David had taken Josh out to a coffee shop, just the two of them. I figured they were going out to get a treat. David sat Josh down in the coffee shop, my boy who was trying so hard, voluntarily, to be the man of the house, and told him he wanted to marry his mom. He asked Josh if he was okay with it and if he was okay with him moving into the role of being his dad on earth. Josh was on board and gave David his approval, which meant David had the green light to plan the dreamy proposal.

The boys were still occasionally sleeping in my bed. That night they both fell asleep in my room while the babysitter was there. When I got home, I crawled into bed with them. I assumed all would be great in the morning and they would be just as excited as I was. Well, I was wrong. When we woke up, Josh saw the engagement ring on my finger. Before I said anything, he immediately pointed to my ring and said, "What is that?!" I excitedly began to tell him about the previous night. He cut me off, yelled at me, left the room, and slammed the door. Jason followed suit.

I was completely caught off guard. Change had been hard for them for obvious reasons, but I was certain they would be just as ecstatic as I was when it came for this change. They loved David, had already bonded with his kids, and everything was going great.

We had a yelling match with many tears that lasted quite some time. I was sad and confused. After we all calmed down, I finally got it out of Josh as to why he was so upset. He was mad that he was not there at the proposal. What?! All that craziness, and that was his issue? I let out a sigh of relief. I could breathe again. We sat down together, and I showed him the pictures I had on my phone. After giving him all the details of our evening, it calmed him down a little bit, and he felt more involved.

That same day, David told Brayden and Tegan the big news. They approved of their dad's decision and were excited. Now that the word was out to the kids, we could share our news with our families and close friends. The closest people to us were ecstatic. They knew how far we both had come. They knew our relationship was built on Christ. They knew we had made each decision with our children in every forethought. They saw the sparkle back in both our eyes and knew at this point in our lives, we were made for each other.

The blessings from our biggest fans and prayer warriors were more confirmation I was taking my next steps in the right direction. Even so, I still held so much worry and fear. It took a little while for me to be okay with sharing our news publicly. I was still in a spot where I was worried about judgment from others. Will they think I do not still love Mike? Will they think we are moving too fast? Will I be looked at as selfish and not doing what was best for my boys? Will they think David is crazy for taking on the three of us? My feelings weren't unfounded, as some people did feel that way and voiced their opinions to me directly and behind my back as well.

Once again, working through my feelings in therapy, through prayer and guidance from our biggest supporters, I was able to shake those feelings. I had lost my husband at age thirty-three. He was my first and only love, my best friend, the father of my children, my future, my provider, my everything. Never in a million years did I think he would be taken from me before we were ninety. During the days and the year following his death, I never thought I would love again. I thought my life was over and my future was gone.

When you experience something as sudden and traumatic as I did, your perspectives on life and love change. I viewed the world, the boys' and my lives, and what God's plan was for us through a completely new and vastly different lens. Marrying David was what God had planned for the boys and me. Even more so, I knew that Mike would approve. That is all that mattered to me.

This time around, the wedding planning would be quite different. When Mike and I got married at twenty-one in a big church, my Cinderella wedding dreams were all fulfilled, complete with a horse-drawn carriage waiting for us outside the church. Fourteen years later I didn't really care to be Cinderella or make a big fuss about anything. I only cared to walk down the aisle with my boys on either side of me to David and his kids waiting for us. I couldn't wait to promise to love and cherish him for all the days of my life. I just wanted to begin our last chapter together with our blended family of six. I knew the rest would fall into place, and it did.

We knew we wanted something small, simple, outdoors, and preferably in a country-like setting. We looked at place after place close to the area where we lived. Nothing felt right. Then, on a visit to see my parents in Nevada, we spent a day sightseeing, and I showed him all around my old stomping grounds. We were enjoying a glass of wine at a beautiful location where I worked in high school, David Walley's Hot Springs in Genoa. It didn't take long before we both knew this was it. We had found the place where we would become husband and wife.

The wedding planning was easy and for the most part stress free. The resort took care of everything. We just had to create our small guest list, shop for wedding dresses for Tegan and me, rent suits for David and our three boys, and add some rustic chic touches to the décor. Everything was simple, elegant, and absolutely perfect.

With it being a destination wedding, we got to spend the weekend with the closest people in our lives. We didn't need a big rehearsal or a rehearsal dinner, so we took time to enjoy the Friday before the big day. The boys went fishing, and we girls had our nails done and relaxed. As more of our family and friends arrived, we got to visit and hang out together. At the end of the day, David and I said our goodbyes as we parted ways to our own rooms, he with his kids and me with mine. We decided David and I wouldn't see each other again until we did our first look with the photographer.

The morning of our wedding day, April 28, 2018, Josh and Jason went to David's room to get ready with him and Brayden. Tegan came to get ready with me. I know the four of them had their share of laughs and bonding as they got ready for the big day. We girls had a day I will forever cherish. I had always dreamed of having a daughter. David's daughter and I formed a bond early on. The first day I met her we clicked. She was instantly the daughter I never had. The day we spent together getting our hair and makeup done, getting dressed together, and taking pictures will always be one of my most precious memories.

Our wedding was scheduled for early evening. After a long day of getting ready, it was time for David and me to meet up alone to have our first look with the photographer. I will never forget the butterflies I had as I walked up to him, his back turned to me. I tapped him on the shoulder, and as he turned around, he stared at me in awe and told me I looked beautiful. As soon as I saw his handsome face and he wrapped his arms around me, all the nervousness I felt instantly disappeared. After we had our moment and took our own pictures, all the kids joined in for family pictures. These pictures will forever be treasured, as it was the day we blended our families together as one.

Blending a family is not easy. It is not very natural either. When blending a family, a choice has been made to combine two sets of worlds together into one. Building a strong foundation in the beginning is key. David and I recognized this early on and decided to design our wedding ceremony around blending our new family of six, not just focusing on the two of us joining in marriage. Even with me being the daddy's girl I am and having my dad be one of David's and my biggest fans, I decided my boys would walk me down the aisle and give me away. Waiting at the altar with David was Brayden, who was his best man, and Tegan, who was my maid of honor and flower girl.

Our pastor asked the question, "Who gives this woman to be married to this man?" and Josh replied, "My brother and I do." Then he placed my hand in David's. Josh stood next to his new sister, and Jason stood next to his new brother. We strategically placed the kids so that it was obvious to them and our guests there was not his side or her side; all was ours.

We wrote vows to our children. We shared in the reading of these vows and took turns making our serious and funny promises to each of them. The vows read:

> *David: We wrote these vows for you as promises of how we intend to lead and raise you in the ways of our Lord.*
> *April: When we made our commitment to be together forever it was with ALL six of us in mind, not just David and myself. With lots of prayer and God's direction we made the decision to become a family of six; not his kids or my kids anymore, you are OUR kids.*
> *David: With God in the center of our family, I promise to raise you boys with honor and respect for your dad, loving you as my own, in hopes of always making him proud.*
> *April: You two are very blessed to have an amaz-*

ing mom. I promise to come alongside her and your dad to help them raise you two, also as my own, and with God as our center.

David and April: We promise to love and respect each other as God has designed us to. We pray that our example of marriage and how we treat each other will teach you how to love and respect each other as brothers and sister. We pray this is true not only with each other but with friends, family, and anyone who may cross your path.

David: I promise to lead our family with fun and adventure. Camping, fishing, dirt-bike riding, and sports will always be a part of this family. I promise to have lots of Nerf wars, just don't tell your mom.

April: And I promise to bake lots of brownies. I promise to never stop telling you how much I love you or stop kissing all of your cute faces. Even when you four are grown up, I'll continue to embarrass you with my "I love you mores" and kissy faces. And I promise to always make you clean up your Nerf bullets.

David: At times you guys may not understand the way we discipline and parent. But we pray Proverbs 22:6 over you: "Direct your children onto the right path, and when they are older, they will not leave it." We pray God will always be the center of and lead your lives. We love you.

David and I went on to take communion, and we had the

children join us. At this time, our pastor's wife came up and prayed over our family. We continued the ceremony with sharing our vows with each other and exchanging the rings, which David's best man, his son, was holding for us. My vows read:

David,

I love you more than any words could describe. Today, this wedding, this moment, is so sacred and special. Not too long ago you were just a dream and a prayer. A down-on-my-knees, crying-out-for-God-to-save-me kind of prayer that I never knew if and when God would answer. And this day, the Lord has heard the cry of my heart and has answered my prayers. You, babe, are truly heaven sent.

I promise to put God first in my life and our marriage. To encourage and even challenge you in your walk with the Lord, as well as in all areas of life. I promise to show you respect and allow you to lead our family as God leads you. I promise to always do my best to be your helpmate, your biggest cheerleader, your prayer warrior, and your best friend.

I will attempt to cook you yummy meals, take care of the chores at home, and do all I can to make our beautiful house a place you can't wait to come home to at the end of each day. Twix bars, flowers, and taking me to Giants games will definitely help with that too.

I promise to always have a sense of humor. To laugh with you and to laugh at you. I won't sweat the small stuff, and I will always communicate to you how I am feeling. I know firsthand how extremely precious life is. I promise to never forget that. I promise to never go to bed angry and to always kiss you goodbye. I will cherish every moment with you as if it's our last and never ever stop telling you how much you mean to me, how much I love you, and that you are my answered prayer and my dream come true.

We were not told of something amazing, which happened during this moment, until the reception, and neither of us had even noticed. While I was reading my vows to David and read the line, "I will always kiss you goodbye," a motorcycle cop drove by on the country road above where our ceremony was taking place. The roar of the motorcycle can even be heard in our wedding video. The craziest part is that typically motors officers do not work on the weekends, and there may be one or possibly two in my tiny hometown. Out of all the times and places for one to be driving by, it was at the exact moment in our wedding ceremony when I was telling my new husband on earth how much I will always appreciate him because I lost my first love, my husband in heaven. It was as if Mike were there with us, driving by and giving his approval.

Next David read his vows to me:

Vows to My Beautiful Wife
April, I love you beyond what these words can express.

I thank God every morning and night for crossing our paths.

It seems like just a short time ago you were just a prayer, one that I asked God for every day. Those prayers were answered even more than I could have imagined.

God has blessed me with most beautiful, smart, hardworking, faithful, God-centered woman.

With my whole heart, I gladly take you as my wife, accepting your strengths, weaknesses, family, and friends, just as you do mine.

I promise to support you, protect you, lead you, and love you always—as God has commanded.

I promise to always tell you how much I love you, how beautiful you are, and to always kiss you goodbye before work.

I will be your rock through the good times and the bad.

I promise to always communicate with you, never letting the sun go down on our anger.

I will love your boys as my own, leading them to God every step of the way.

I promise to forever honor and respect the amazing husband you once had, the amazing father to your boys. I will do my best to always keep those memories alive and present in our new blended family.

I promise to always support you in honoring his name and legacy through any path you choose.

April, the love you have shown me and my kids is amazing, but after meeting your family it doesn't surprise me that you love the way you do.

I stand here this evening in awe of your beauty inside and out.

Just a short time ago I questioned God. I was angry because I thought He didn't hear my prayers or care to answer them. But as always He provided and answered my prayers. He provided you, my wife and best friend. He provided a spouse perfect in every way, only He could have ordained.

April, I love you, and I can say that I am truly blessed to walk through life with you as husband and wife!

As our wedding ceremony came to an end, it was finally official; we were not just husband and wife, but we were now a family. To us, our wedding ceremony was perfect. We achieved our goal of including our children, which made for such an intimate and special celebration. Next, it was time to party.

"Now introducing . . . Mr. and Mrs. David Redgrave!" the DJ announced, as we made our way through the double doors into our beautiful reception venue. The intimate, beautiful glass-walled gazebo was filled with our family and some of our closest friends. The sun was setting, twinkle lights hung from the ceiling, candles were lit, and lanterns were glowing. We made our way while holding hands and smiling from ear to ear to the front of the room to join our wedding party . . . our four children.

The six of us stood together in front of the candlelit mantle of the brick fireplace. A section of candles was black with blue lace wrapped around them to symbolize Mike. David and our three boys had changed out of their dress shoes into casual shoes with a thin, blueline flag with Mike's initials and badge number painted on them, which David had made for each of them. Our guests were still on their feet cheering and welcoming us in for the party to begin. It was time for that special song to be played for the traditional first dance. Yet, this first song was not going to be played for the first dance of my husband and me. This first dance, this moment was for my boys and me.

David took the mic, and with heartfelt tears, he shared why he wouldn't be my first dance at our wedding.

"Before I have the first dance with my wife, I want to do something a little different that God has been pressing on my heart. At first, I was worried about sharing this idea with April and worried about what people would think. But I knew that none of that mattered. All that mattered was doing something to show Josh and Jason that their Dad will always be honored and respected. He will always be a part of this new blended family. Never diminished or forgotten.

"Before I dance with my wife for the first time, Josh and Jason will get the opportunity to dance with their mom. This represents a passing of the torch from the boys to me. They have done such a good job of protecting and taking care of their mom, and now I get to take over and fill that role. Most importantly, I see it as a way for their father to have one last dance with their mom before I take the role of husband, earthly father, and leader of this beautiful, blended family. Hoping and praying to succeed in making Mike proud of the husband and father I become.

The song we chose for this dance is 'Tell Your Heart to Beat Again.' This song means so much to both me and April. At the same exact time in our lives we needed the words and truth in this song to pick up the pieces of our shattered hearts and learn to live and love again. Only God knew what we needed and where He'd bring us. With faith, trust, and relentless prayer, we both stand here tonight in awe of how far He brought us and our family of six."

There were tears and laughter shared between each of my sons and me as we danced. It was a moment I hope they always remember as a way we not only honored their dad and the beautiful marriage he and I had, but to also feel that sense of relief. Relief in knowing that they didn't have to feel as if they had to be the men of the house anymore. That sense of relief knowing that their mom was going to be okay, loved, and taken care of. The burden of feeling as if they needed to protect and care for me as they had seen their dad do was lifted. Their dad on earth could now take that load off their shoulders. It was a moment the three of us will never forget.

Chapter 16

◆

Becoming Seven

Many newly married couples hop on a plane a day or two after their wedding and jet off to their anticipated honeymoon. David and I went big and planned the most amazing honeymoon to Bora Bora, complete with a bungalow over the French Polynesian waters, but we had to wait almost a week before we could jet off. Days after marrying my husband on earth and becoming his wife, I had to turn my focus back on being the widow of Officer Katherman by attending the annual San Jose Police Department Fallen Officer ceremony to honor my husband in heaven. My dual role of being a wife and a widow began immediately.

The months started to fly by as we settled into our new life of being a blended family of six. Our new house started to become home, we had all the kids at the same private school, and sports schedules took over our afternoons, evenings, and weekends. I, still home with the kids and not yet returning to teaching, was managing it all during the days while David was at work. As much as we were all comfortable and happy with how life was flowing, there was still something missing. That something turned into another one of our greatest leaps of faith.

About five months after losing Mike, I had the most vivid dream. A dream I never really understood, yet I knew there was great significance to it. In this dream I was on a walk with a little girl. A petite, blonde toddler walking in front of me. I never saw her face, only the back of her. She was wearing a cute pink summer dress and sandals, and her blonde hair was flowing in the breeze. In my dream I knew she was my daughter. The only thing I did in this dream was follow behind my little girl as she giggled and skipped down a path.

I remember waking up and being stunned at how real the dream was and a little bummed thinking that would never be me. All I knew and believed was that God's plan was for me to be a boy mom and a mom of two. Having a daughter was always something I had wondered about. If Mike and I would have tried for number three, would it have been a girl? We would joke saying, "With our luck it would be twin boys."

I didn't have the easiest of pregnancies with my sons. They were also both born premature. With that to consider, as well as the nature of Mike's line of work and the crazy schedule he always had, we made the decision not to have any more children after Jason was born. We went as far as having a tubal ligation done during my C-section. So this dream of me walking with a daughter was just that, a dream. Not only had we made the decision to not have any more children, let alone a little girl, my husband was gone. It was now my two sons and me. I couldn't imagine having any more children who would have to face losing their dad. I started to understand why God's plan was for me to have only two . . . or so I thought.

Fast-forward to our new blended family life, and I was instantly a mom and bonus mom of four. My two boys were thriving, and Brayden and Tegan had brought even more joy and love into my life. When I met Tegan, I thought back to the dream I had. Maybe this was my dream unfolding. God was blessing me with a daughter. Yet, Tegan was five when I met her, not a toddler. In the back of my mind, I never thought I would be having any more children of my own.

David and I started to seriously discuss and pray about the idea of having more children. We knew it wouldn't be an easy feat and may not even be a possibility. After lots of prayer and consideration, we decided that we would reach out to my doctors, get their opinions, and go from there. The verdict was that doing a tubal ligation reversal was not an option for me. We were referred to an Invitro Fertilization (IVF) doctor to weigh our options. We were still unsure about everything and not clear on what God's plan was either. We decided that we would both go ahead and do the necessary testing needed for an initial consultation with an IVF doctor.

We were nervous and didn't know what to expect. We were not fully educated on the whole IVF process. I remember going into the consultation full of hope and excitement and leaving deflated. Basically, the tests results showed my body was already in a premenopausal state. I didn't have very many eggs, and our chance of IVF being successful was about 4 percent. Apparently, going through the hormone changes of a tubal ligation at the young age of twenty-five, combined with all the trauma my body went through when I lost Mike, played a pretty hefty toll on me. The news was disappointing. We were out of options to conceive a baby, and I felt like it was all my fault.

Throughout my life, and especially after the hell and high water I had gone through, God had proven Himself repeatedly to be more than faithful. Even through my darkest and most challenging times, He performed numerous miracles and knocked my socks off with blessing after blessing. So, when the doctors told me I had a 4 percent chance of getting pregnant through the IVF process, I definitely felt discouraged at first. Ultimately, I knew my God was bigger than any percentage or statistic I was given. David and I decided we would begin the long process of IVF and see where it led us. There were multiple steps in the process, and we knew God would either open or close doors for us throughout our journey to be a family of seven.

With each step, and even to the doctors' surprise, we would receive good news, and our percentage rate of success would ever-so-slightly increase. As the months went on, the appointments, blood tests, ultrasounds, and shots became more frequent. All of this eventually led up to multiple procedures of egg retrieval, fertilization period, freezing embryos, genetic testing, and implantation. God was faithful, and He proved the doctors wrong each step of the way.

There were many times throughout the process when I wanted to give up because I didn't think I was strong enough to continue. At one point I was giving myself seven shots a day. I was sore, bruised, sick, and emotional. It took a toll on my body. Then I had to remind myself that my God is stronger than me, and if He kept opening another door through this process, I would keep putting my faith and trust in His plan for our family.

There was a lot of hurry-up-and-wait throughout the IVF process. The final procedure was implanting our embryo. We made the decision to implant one embryo, the strongest embryo regardless of the sex. There is about a two-week waiting period before getting the results of a pregnancy. I wanted to know the outcome so badly, yet I also didn't want to know at all due to fear of failure. I didn't think I could go through the process all over again if the results were negative. I was so scared to get bad news because I couldn't bear another loss.

The day I was expecting that important phone call happened to be the same day I was to attend the annual San Jose Police Department Fallen Officer memorial ceremony for Mike. The same exact ceremony we attended a year prior and had to postpone our anticipated honeymoon for. I was already a little anxious and emotional because the ceremony, as honoring and beautiful as it is, is always difficult for me to attend. Now at any moment I would be receiving the news which could very well turn a difficult day into an incredibly happy one or a difficult day into an even harder one. All in one day I was once again portraying the role of wife, mom, widow, and hopefully, newly expecting. God's timing is something I will never understand. I know His timing is perfect yet sometimes so hard to comprehend. Of all days, why would I be getting this news today? Yet, He knows me so well and knew I needed something good to be associated with this ceremony I will attend every year.

His timing was perfect. An hour after the ceremony, I received the call. My blood test results came back positive. Our embryo had successfully implanted, and I was officially pregnant. The wait was over, and God preformed another miracle in my life, in my body. He also never fails to have another gift up His sleeve and in His plan. The embryo we implanted was a girl. We were having a baby girl. My vivid dream I had five months after losing Mike was starting to unfold. David and I were elated and so beyond amazed at how God continued to prove Himself faithful to us.

Telling the kids I was pregnant, that they were getting a baby sister, had to be creative and fun. We took some time to brainstorm what we were going to do. Our special and specifically-tailored-to-each-kid announcements were a hit, and we now had extremely excited big brothers and a big sister.

This pregnancy was much like my other two. Lots of extra monitoring, ultrasounds, and shots to prevent preterm labor. My body just does not want to keep a baby in full-term. Tuesday morning of December 12 was going to be a busy morning. I had multiple appointments back-to-back for my thirty-six-week checkups. After getting the kids off to school, I headed to the hospital in Santa Clara. First, I had my twice-a-week pregnancy nonstress test. Then, an anatomy scan ultrasound on the baby, an appointment with my high-risk doctor, followed by an appointment with the doctor scheduled to do my C-section planned for December 30. My plan was to get through all my appointments in time to pick up the kids from school, meet my parents who were driving from Nevada to visit, and get the family to Tegan's Christmas program in the evening.

God had quite different plans for our day. The nonstress test showed I was having contractions. I did feel a little off and crampy that morning, but I was so focused on my busy day, I was not paying attention to what my body was telling me. As I went on to the ultrasound, baby girl looked good yet was still breech and in an extremely uncomfortable position. The cramping got worse as I walked down the halls to my next appointment where my doctor confirmed I had started to dilate. As I moved on to the next appointment, I kept convincing myself I was fine because I needed to get back home. Sure enough, the doctor sent me to Labor and Delivery. Luckily, I was already at the hospital because by the time I walked over to that department, my contractions were two to three minutes apart, and I had dilated more. I was not going to make it to pick up the kids from school or get to the Christmas program. It was early, but it was time to have this baby.

It was a long afternoon and evening of contractions, and dialing in the right pain meds, until it was finally my turn to be taken back for surgery. Apparently, the night before Friday the thirteenth and a full moon means everyone goes into labor at the same time. Almost twelve years prior, I had a C-section with Jason. I somewhat knew what to expect this time around, yet I was still nervous. After I was all prepped and David joined me, the surgery went quick. Before we knew it, we were hearing our precious little girl crying. The birth plan was to bring her to me for skin-to-skin time. As I laid on the table, I kept waiting for them to bring her back over to me, but it never happened.

I intuitively knew something was not right. The NICU doctor was called in immediately, and the team of nurses and doctors were quiet. I could tell there was something wrong. Due to her breech position, my baby girl appeared to have deformities in her face, which raised the question of neurological issues. I never got to see her face, but according to her daddy and the surgical team, it was obvious something was not right. Thank goodness the NICU doctor was already brought in because she was also struggling to breathe on her own. Rather quickly she was put into the incubator and taken to the NICU. David went with her while my surgery was completed and I was sent to recovery.

I didn't even get to see my little girl. Our parents and the four kids were in the waiting room and so eager to meet their new granddaughter and baby sister. Unfortunately, they all went home with no one getting to meet her. The surgery was tough on me, and it took longer than expected for me to get out of recovery. I was not going to be able to see her in the NICU until I was stable. Finally, the next day around ten in the morning, they let David wheel me over to the NICU to meet our baby girl for the first time. Both my boys were born early. Earlier than her at thirty-four and thirty-five weeks, but neither of them had any issues. Even though this was my longest-term baby, it was my first experience with the NICU.

She was so tiny and covered in tubes. Breathing tube, feeding tube, an IV, and lots of wired monitors made it hard to even see what she looked like. It was difficult to see my precious baby in that condition. I felt so helpless, but with the help of the amazing nurses, we were able to maneuver all her tubes and wires for me to finally hold her for the first time.

Thank the Lord the facial deformities went away over the next couple of days. The fluid in her lungs had caused her respiratory issues. We spent the next seven days visiting her in the NICU. After I was discharged on day four, we were extremely fortunate to get a room in the NICU so we could stay close to her. Unfortunately, no children under fourteen were allowed in, so her anxious big brothers and sister never got to meet her in the hospital.

Over those seven days, she got stronger each day. Once we finally got to take her home to her brothers and sister, our journey to becoming a family of seven was finally complete.

I would sit in our home holding this beautiful baby girl. As I would stare at her precious face, I couldn't help but feel contentment and joy. My healing had come full circle. Tears that would once stream down my face in agony, heartache, and pain were now streams of overwhelming joy and love for this little miracle and dream come true wrapped in pink, who I get to call mine, my daughter.

As always, I was concerned and worried about how Josh and Jason would adjust to their little sister. Would it stir up any emotions of grief because this new sibling was from David and me and not their dad and me? Would they be mad at me? Would they love her as their sister? Once again, God is bigger than any worry or doubt I ever have and proves to me, as He always does, that He is in control, and His plan was and is perfect. Josh and Jason adore their baby sister. They are loving, sweet, gentle, and protective of her. Same goes for Brayden and Tegan. These kids have adored their baby sister from day one. She was not only a gift from God to me and David, but to her big brothers and sister as well.

Can I say that all these amazing blessings I have been given have made the healing process of my grief complete? Absolutely not. I will be working through my stages of grief most likely for the rest of my life. I know that I can have both though. I can both grieve the loss and love I have for Mike and love David too. I can miss Mike while I stare into the eyes of my daughter and be thankful for this new life. I live my life each day hoping to make Mike proud. I hope and pray he is looking down at Josh, Jason, and me, nodding his head and saying, "Good job, good job," just as he did in my dream.

Epilogue

On Faith and Loss

I have persevered through some agonizing trials that have tested my faith. I thought I could handle anything by this point, but the evening of my C-section, when my little girl was wheeled out without my seeing her and then having to watch her struggle to breathe in the NICU, ranked high up on the testing-of-my-faith scale. Yet David and I knew God was taking care of her; God was taking care of us. Just conceiving her was a miracle, let alone having her finally with us, NICU or not. It was our faith in Christ that was our strength.

Faith is complete trust in or confidence in someone or something. Faith is trusting in something you cannot explicitly prove. Faith is substance of things hoped for and the evidence things exist that are not yet perceived. Faith is trusting in the unknown even when all hope has been lost. So, when something happens in life that completely rocks your world and turns it upside down, how is it possible to have faith? A loss of a relationship shatters your trust; a loss of a loved one breaks your heart; health challenges deteriorate your hope. Any type of loss in life will affect faith. Faith in Christ, faith in love, and faith in life itself.

For me, I ultimately knew God was in control when my husband died, as horrible as it was, with my world shattered and my heart broken. Sure, I questioned my faith in Christ and was angry at God for letting such tragedy happen to our family. Yet, even with all those questions, I remained faithful knowing God would take care of us. The part of my faith I struggled with the most was my faith in love. I had lost the love of my life when I lost my husband. I felt as if my future had been taken from me. I didn't know if I would ever love again. There are no guarantees in life.

Getting your faith back after any type of loss takes a conscious effort and a choice to search deep and rediscover trust, hope, and confidence that was once there. But it's scary, I know, because something you had was taken away. It's hard to imagine life can be as great as it once was. For me, it was scary when I went on my first date with David because my faith in love was gone. It was scary when we got more serious, made the decision to marry, and blend our families because the faith I once had for my future was gone. It was scary when we decided to go through with the IVF process and attempt to have a baby because I didn't want to possibly bear another loss. But with each step forward, my faith was renewed.

My ultimate faith in Christ never left. In fact, faith is the only thing that has gotten me to the place where I am today. Where the shattered pieces of love and life have been put back together. A place where I can share even in my darkest days, living out my worst nightmare, experiencing my own deepest hell on earth. This is where I was able to find my faith again.

My baby girl is healthy, beautiful, and my dream come true. Savannah Faith is our miracle and a testimony to God's perfect plan for our lives, even when we lost all hope. The little girl from my dream, light-colored hair and all, is now a part of my life, and she makes each day brighter.

No matter what your loss may be—a marriage, friendship, employment, health, death—when all faith and hope feel lost in the moment of your heartbreak, I promise, they are still there. Be brave. Make the choice to find them and believe.

The ashes of my life were in piles. Big heaping piles. Yet God has been gradually cleaning up those ashes and turning the soot into pure beauty. Through hell and high water, I have given, and always will give, all the praise and glory to my Lord for bringing me through great tragedy into amazing love, all the while honoring my husband in heaven, Michael Jason Katherman.

A Note from David Redgrave

Before I met April, my life had recently been flipped upside down. One day after work, I came home and made my way upstairs like any normal day. But this day was different. This time the house was cleaned out, my kids were not there, and it was eerily silent. As I made my way to my bedroom, my worst nightmare started to unfold.

As a Christian, I didn't think about divorce very often. In my mind, it would never happen to me. Unfortunately, I was wrong. My wife had packed all her clothes and belongings and moved out. My kids were already with their grandma in anticipation of an exceedingly difficult and heated conversation that began on the "D" word. The house was empty, the bank account split, and divorce papers drafted, all while I had no clue.

During the conversation, my mind was racing, and my body went numb. All I could think was, this couldn't really be happening. How would I get on living my life without my wife of nine years? I couldn't help but be severely angry about being forced to now be a part-time dad. No matter what I said or how much I begged and pleaded, this was happening. Nothing was going to change her mind.

The following months were difficult for me. I couldn't count the number of arguments trying to get her to see things my way, trying to convince her things could work out. We started seeing a Christian counselor but for vastly different reasons. In my mind, I saw this as a way we could save a sinking ship. Unfortunately, for her, it was a way to seek counsel on how to co-parent in this very real and new life.

Throughout our time in counseling, I fell into a deep depression. The days flew by, but nothing was memorable. My routine became wake up, drive to work, have no appetite, come home, curl up in bed, and do nothing. I had no drive to live my life. The many nights I spent alone without my kids were the toughest. Negative thoughts flooded my mind: I wasn't good enough. I was a horrible father and husband. Eventually I started to believe all the lies flooding my mind.

One night, in a very depressed state, I decided to get in my truck and drive. At first, I didn't know where I was going or what I was going to do. I began screaming at God. *How could you let this happen to me? Why won't you change her mind? Why will you not fix this relationship, this family?* The thought of not seeing my kids each day, only getting them half of the time—if I was lucky—started to haunt me even more. My weakness began to be preyed upon with each minute that passed by until I finally snapped and couldn't take it anymore.

I pulled my truck into a dark and deserted parking lot. I was alone. No other cars and no light to make me visible. I turned off my truck and sobbed to God. Thoughts of ending my own life were real. I told God I didn't want to live this life anymore. To this point, I still had not told anyone of the reality of my ending marriage, and I sure didn't want to face the music. I was in a very weak and frail state. The negative thoughts grew heavier and heavier until they were too much to take. I made one last plea to God.

With the little faith I had left, I begged for God to let me know I would be okay, and that my kids would be okay. I begged Him to show me a clear sign and pull me from this wreckage. I would never question Him again. I promised to live and let go and allow Him to guide my every way from here on out.

No more than ten seconds later, He provided this for me. An owl landed on the hood of my truck. This owl seemed so calm and powerful. This owl sat there staring at me with glowing eyes. I looked directly into this owl's eyes and knew God was there. I knew He would see me through my hell.

The following weeks and months were different. The many things weighing me down no longer did. I reached out and began to heal through telling friends and family my situation. The final step was allowing myself to accept the reality my spouse I was fighting for was not going to change her mind. I began to let go. I began to gain my relationship with God again. My faith grew stronger by the day. Further down that road of healing, I began to gain more confidence. Maybe I would be good enough for someone again. Maybe I was not a horrible father or spouse. I knew I wanted to be in a relationship but didn't know how or when it would be.

One day I finally made the decision to put myself out there. I decided to try an online dating website. This was *not* me, and to be honest, I used to make fun of people who joined these sites. I was still healing and was in no way going to try and meet someone at parties, bars, or random events. After all, I was just getting back enough energy to do things outside of the house.

I made an online profile and decided, out of respect for my ex-wife, I was not going to put any pictures on my profile. What kind of crazy woman would decide to talk to a guy with no pictures? After a couple of days scrolling through profiles, I came across one that seemed so different. This woman was so naturally beautiful and modest. She didn't have thirty pictures of herself chalked full of makeup or in her bikini. In the picture, which caught my attention, she was wearing a hat at a baseball game. Baseball was my life, so this earned her some brownie points! With butterflies and blind courage, I sent her a message. To my astonishment, she responded. Hours of phone conversations getting to know each other followed.

This bit of courage turned into the beautiful life I now have with April. Our road to present day was full of ups and downs with unchartered territory for each of us. Blending families together was not easy. What remained true through all of this was the faithfulness of God. He never left our sides and always brought us more than we could imagine.

The biggest surprise of my relationship with April was finding out who she was. She asked me if I knew who she was eventually after we started talking. My first thought was, wow, this woman is self-centered and full of herself. I was not prepared to hear the reason why she asked. Finding out she was a widow was not the shocker. She had this status on her profile. Finding out why she was a widow and who she was married to was the surprising part.

I remembered hearing her story. I remembered her husband and her tragedy being all over the news. Initially, I didn't know if I was the right man for her. The thoughts of not being good enough crept back in. I began to have questions about her too. My thoughts swirled. What would it be like to date a widow? Would it be harder? Would it be easier? What would other people think? Is she ready to date again? Is she mentally and emotionally capable of loving again?

Simply reminding myself that God is enough and I don't have to be, really helped me through these fears. Dating a widow was not going to scare me away. As a matter of fact, knowing she was a widow and hearing her tell her whole story only made me draw even closer to her. This is where the unconditional love of God helped prepare my heart for a special woman like April.

Dating a widow is like any other relationship in some ways, yet certain aspects can be radically different. Dating April challenged me daily. There were many obstacles, especially with our children. There was a point in our relationship when things started to get a little more serious, and I reached a fork in the road. One way would lead me down a smooth path where there were no hurdles or bumps in the road. This path was the path of avoidance, the choice to end the relationship and cut things off. It would be easier not to deal with all of the baggage April would bring into the relationship. The second road was full of twists, turns, hills, and bumps. As my father-in-law would like to point out, kind of like the horrible California roads, not the smooth roads of Nevada!

This path was daunting and scary. But taking this road head-on has brought me love like I have never experienced. Loving April has challenged me to examine my every move and my every word. It has caused me to fight my instincts that urge me toward the easier option. One struggle I found with April was dealing with her rough days. The days she was really feeling her loss for Mike. It could be a date in the month which matched the date Mike died, or it could just be a day which she was struggling with feeling empty from missing him. Either way, this was foreign territory to me.

A quite different aspect I experienced, and still do, is Mike still being a part of April's everyday life. When she talks about him, she smiles from ear to ear. His pictures are scattered throughout our house. His belongings are in many areas of our house. They may be here for an exceptionally long time, possibly forever. At times this has made me feel downplayed, or even second fiddle. It didn't feel natural to see pictures of April and Mike right next to pictures of her and me. Even though it felt unnatural, I soon learned there was not a threat in the attachment April has to these memories. In no way, shape, or form is it any sort of competition. I know men especially find this hard to deal with, thinking more like competitors than lovers.

I have learned how important it is to allow all of Mike to be present in everyday life, even encouraging April in making sure he is always remembered. This is especially true with her boys being involved. Nothing is more important to me than making sure their dad, whom they no longer have with them, is always remembered and a part of our newly formed family. We put pictures on the mantle. I take the boys to get birthday and holiday gifts for April in honor of what their dad would have done. We go many places they all once enjoyed as a family. We celebrate Mike's birthday in positive ways. I do the best I can to make all memories of Mike positive ones. And lastly, I don't try to hide or get rid of Mike's personal belongings which, to me, may be a nuisance, but many of these items are precious and coveted by April and the boys.

Next, a struggle I faced was judgment and fitting into the existing mold of April's friends and family. It was extremely uncomfortable and awkward meeting her family and friends. I felt judged and the center of debate when meeting them. Now I know it felt the same for April, her family, and friends. They were all grieving and adjusting to life without Mike, which caused many to be cautious and protective. Time washed away all these feelings and formed amazing relationships with equally amazing people.

I thought many people would judge me for dating, falling in love, and marrying a widow. Some people believed that since April lost her husband, she was mentally incapable of being "all there" or genuinely loving another man. I faced all these assumptions myself. I had to trust my heart and what I knew was best. I did my best to ignore what others thought, and soon found out they were completely wrong.

April has a completely different respect for love and life. The little things, which could blow up and cause arguments in normal relationships, are insignificant to her. She knows how trivial these things are. I have been showered with so much love and acts of service, at times I feel guilty. It is her unlimited love which has caused me to reciprocate and love more than I feel capable of. April can love so relentlessly because she knows, unlike anyone else, just how precious life is. She knows one day I may not come home. Loving a widow, and being loved unconditionally in return, is unlike any other love I have experienced.

Being the parent on earth to the boys has its ups and downs. Many times, I struggle with feeling like I am not good enough, like I simply cannot provide what these boys need. Inevitably, I started to have negative thoughts. I started to think if Mike were here, none of their struggles would be an issue. These boys would excel and thrive much better in life. In a post I wrote for April's blog, I talked to Mike about many of my struggles. The words below are some of the things I feel and struggle with.

I know you can see all I struggle with when nobody else does, even April. Believe it or not, coming into the lives of your bride and your boys was an easy decision. I know how you felt about them, and I feel the same way too. What I didn't know was just how much hurt and destruction these three were dealing with. I knew losing you rocked their world, but I was unprepared for what was to come.

My heart hurt on a daily basis knowing what they were going through. I prayed daily for the strength and wisdom to help them the best way I could. I gently and slowly entered their lives out of respect for you and respect for their broken, fragile hearts. The boys have both dealt with the loss of you so differently. With one, trust was hard to gain, and he didn't want his mom further than arm's reach. With the other, it felt as if the trust was there and nothing was wrong. As time moved on, the trust was formed and things began to change.

I thank God that you and I enjoy the same hobbies, sports, and places to adventure. This made the connection with me and your boys so much stronger. The very things we enjoy most, which bring smiles to our faces and forge lasting memories, also bring internal hurt and sadness in me. Sometimes I am stopped dead in my tracks and struck with guilt during fun and positive activities.

My favorite hobby is fishing, and I am glad it was one of yours too. Quite a few times I couldn't help but feel guilt while out on a trip with the boys. In Hawaii, when we were there for your birthday week, I rented our own charter boat to fish offshore for a chance to catch big game fish, something Josh tells me you did all the time. I knew he wanted to catch big game fish like you because he made it well known! While on the trip in Hawaii, we caught plenty of smaller tuna, but the day was wearing thin and still nothing big. Selfishly, I prayed for something big, something to make Josh's dream a reality. Two marlin later, his dreams were fulfilled. I was ecstatic and smiling ear to ear. Then it hit me. Your boys experienced this with me, not you . . . I instantly felt guilt and wished you were there to be doing this with your boys.

Recently, Josh and I went on a five-mile mountain bike ride in the hills. At times it was brutal, but he pushed through, and we got to the peak overlooking the town. I thought of how fun it was and how much he was enjoying it. Yet again, guilt sank in. When I am out coaching and helping them with baseball and basketball, the guilt hits from time to time. It is hard for me to say, but I would give anything for you to be back in my shoes and doing all of this with your family again. Often, I will almost angrily cry out to God and ask, "Why? Why me? Why did these boys have to endure so much loss and pain? Why do they have to grow up without their dad? Why do I get to experience all these great memories with them?" I know it is not my place to question God. I may never know why. I have to remind myself, despite all of the burdens and pains those three have dealt with and continue to deal with, my job is to be present and love and lead them.

Being the parent on earth is both a blessing and a curse. It is a huge responsibility. For as much work, for as much pain, for as much blood, sweat, and tears as it may be, it is one of the most rewarding things I have ever experienced. To see a smile on their faces once again. To see them play and act like normal kids again. To see them push past fears and struggles which once held them back. To hear them accidentally call me "Dad." To have them want me at every sporting event, to coach and to teach. To see them live and love again. To see them grow and succeed in life. All of these are some of the most rewarding things life brings.

My life has endured much pain and suffering. It is what I have chosen to do and how I have reacted that has shaped me. I know in the middle of my storm I felt as if I needed to control everything for it to go well. For it to go as I wanted, which was the issue. When I finally let go of the steering wheel and let God take control, it all started to fall into place. When we are in the eye of the storm, in the middle of our trials and tribulations, it is nearly impossible to see any sort of positive outcome. It is nearly impossible to see God's hand at work.

It was further down the road, when I looked back to see how all my struggles have brought me to where I am today. I never could have imagined the amazing life I have now. In the middle of my storm, I thought life was over. I thought nobody would ever want the damaged vessel that I had become. Through a lot of trust and faith, I was able to come out the other end to reap all the benefits He has blessed me with today.

All life's struggles, sufferings, and pain will pass. When it does, the joy life holds for you will be clear. I leave you with these words of encouragement, my favorite Bible verse. A verse I held tightly and reflected upon in times of need.

Isaiah 40:31 ESV, "But they who wait for the Lord shall renew their strength; they shall mount up with wings like eagles; they shall run and not be weary they shall walk and not faint."

~ David Redgrave

About the Author

April prays you will find encouragement and hope through her story, God's story. She has been through the unimaginable. The Lord has brought her through to the other side of a tunnel where there was once no light to be seen. The Lord had and still has a plan for her life, as He does for yours too.

Follow April through her Beauty for Our Ashes ministry where she writes about grief, blending families, love after loss, updates on her life, words of encouragement and hope, and much more.

Visit Beauty for Our Ashes website:
www.beautyforourashes.com

Subscribe to April's blog:
www.beautyforourashes.com/blog/

Follow April on Facebook:
www.facebook.com/Beautyforourashes/

Follow April on Instagram:
www.instagram.com/beautyforourashesblog/

April lives in Gilroy, California, with David, her husband on earth, and their five children, Joshua, Jason, Brayden, Tegan, and Savannah. Because raising the kids keeps her busy, she decided it would be wise to take a break from her career in education. She couldn't be more blessed to be able to stay home and focus her attention on their children. Josh and Jason are now teenagers. They are happy and thriving. Their dad would be so proud.

They call themselves the RedKat Fam, a wonderful blend of the Redgrave and Katherman families. They enjoy exploring the outdoors, fishing, dirt bike riding, four-wheeling, sports, traveling, hosting family and friends at their home, and spending quality time together at their family cabin. As a family, they continue to honor and always remember Mike in everything they do.

Order Information

REDEMPTION **P**
P R E S S

To order additional copies of this book, please visit
www.redemption-press.com.
Also available on Amazon.com and BarnesandNoble.com
or by calling toll-free 1-844-2REDEEM.

CPSIA information can be obtained
at www.ICGtesting.com
Printed in the USA
LVHW110744080521
686862LV00014B/144

9 781646 452279